AMERICAN BOTANICAL PAINTINGS

Native Plants of the Mid Atlantic

A book for artists and gardeners

Edited by Bonnie S. Driggers

Botanical Artists for Education & the Environment

Lydia Inglett Ltd. Publishing

AMERICAN BOTANICAL PAINTINGS

Native Plants of the Mid Atlantic

A book for artists and gardeners

Edited by Bonnie S. Driggers

Botanical Artists for Education & the Environment

Lydia Inglett Ltd. Publishing

Half title page painting: Oakleaf Hydrangea by Barbara Jaynes.
Title page painting: Possumhaw Viburnum by Mary Page Hickey.
Copyright page paintings: Flame Azalea by Holly Maillet,
Wavy-lined Emerald moth by Kandy Phillips,
Small Cabbage White Butterfly by Margaret Farr.
Contents page painting: Bumblebee by Kandy Phillips.

American Botanical Paintings
Native Plants of the Mid Atlantic

A book for artists and gardeners

ISBN: 978-1-938417-11-5

Copyright © 2014 Botanical Artists for Education & the Environment
www.baeecorp.org

Published by Lydia Inglett Ltd. Publishing
www.lydiainglett.com
301 Central Ave. #181
Hilton Head Island, SC 29926
info@starbooks.biz

All rights reserved. No portion of this book may be reproduced, stored in a retrieval system, or transmitted in any form, or by any mean – mechanical, electronic, photocopying, recording, or otherwise – without prior written permission from the publisher, except as provided by United States of America copyright law. Printed in China.

To order more copies of this or any of our books, visit our online bookstore at

The place for beautiful, thoughtful gift books

CONTENTS

Foreword	6
Preface	7
Acknowledgments	8
Introduction	10

PLANT PAINTINGS

Adam's Needle	12		Mountain Laurel	72
American Beautyberry	14		Mountain Woodsorrel	74
American Witchhazel	16		Muscadine	76
Azure Bluet	18		Oakleaf Hydrangea	78
Birdfoot Violet	20		Pawpaw	80
Black Walnut	22		Pickerelweed	82
Blackeyed Susan	24		Pink Azalea	84
Blue Wild Indigo	26		Possumhaw Viburnum	86
Broadleaf Cattail	28		Purple Pitcher Plant	88
Canadian Wildginger	30		Riverbank Grape	90
Cardinalflower	32		Roundleaf Greenbrier	92
Cinnamon Fern	34		Royal Fern	94
Common Persimmon	36		Showy Lady's Slipper	96
Common Winterberry	38		Showy Orchid	98
Crimsoneyed Rosemallow	40		Skunk Cabbage	100
Crossvine	42		Smooth Solomon's Seal	102
Curlyheads	44		Southern Arrowwood	104
Dense Blazing Star	46		Southern Magnolia	106
Downy Rattlesnake Plantain	48		Swamp Milkweed	108
Dwarf Witchalder	50		Sweetgum	110
Eastern Leatherwood	52		Toadshade	112
Eastern Purple Coneflower	54		Tuliptree	114
Eastern Redbud	56		Turk's-cap Lily	116
Flame Azalea	58		Twinleaf	118
Flowering Dogwood	60		Virginia Rose	120
Greek Valerian	62		Virginia Saltmarsh Mallow	122
Highbush Blueberry	64		Virginia Spiderwort	124
Kentucky Lady's Slipper	66		White Fringetree	126
Lizard's Tail	68		Winged Sumac	128
Moccasin Flower	70		Yaupon and Possumhaw	130

Donors	132		References	142
Artists	133		Abbreviations	144
Index of Flora	140		Disclaimer	144
Index of Fauna	141			

Foreword

This book represents the confluence of many important aspects of plants, providing a close look at their innate beauty and exquisite details, as well as rich patterns, forms, and colors. The works, selected from a juried show, were created by some of the finest botanical artists in America. In keeping with the current renaissance of botanical art in the world, these artists recognize the need to inform and inspire people about why these plants matter. Botanical Artists for Education & the Environment demonstrates dedication to teaching more about plants, their conservation, and their complexity, which will lead to a more enlightened understanding of the intrinsic value of plants in our lives.

With a thoughtful focus on mid-Atlantic native plants and their pollinators, the artists depict the plants and some of their pollinators painted with incredible patience and talent. Each plant is accompanied by information to provide greater knowledge and understanding of the plant and its role in nature and gardens. The use of native plants in gardens has many benefits: they are able to withstand the climatic variations of the area; they have an evolved partnership with native pollinators; and they play a critical role in the food web. Native plants contribute to our sense of place, and even those plants we may have taken for granted can be seen in a new light as we fully observe and appreciate them.

The U.S. Botanic Garden was thrilled to be a part of this book as it embodies what we know to be vital – our world is better and richer with fine botanical art, and the plants in our backyards, in our woods, and along the roadsides are amazing!

Holly H. Shimizu
Executive Director
U.S. Botanic Garden

Virginia Rose
by Margaret Farr

Preface

In 2011, a group of artists in the Washington, D.C., area formed a nonprofit corporation called Botanical Artists for Education & the Environment (BAEE). Later that same year the corporation received Federal 501(c)(3) tax-exempt status. All members of the Board of Directors serve as unpaid volunteers. Additional members are participants in the project, including both artists and other supporters. Publication costs come from donations. BAEE will donate proceeds from the sale of the book to nonprofit organizations working on native plant education, conservation, and horticulture.

We decided that working toward a specific goal would inspire us to spend more time painting and thereby improve our artistic skills. After consulting with botanists at the U.S. Botanic Garden (USBG) and at Meadowlark Botanical Gardens in Vienna, Virginia, we chose to paint plants native to the mid Atlantic. We invited other artists, mostly those in the mid-Atlantic region, to participate in a juried competition for inclusion of their work in a book.

The resulting book, *American Botanical Paintings: Native Plants of the Mid Atlantic,* contains 60 reproductions of original botanical paintings and drawings; a number of original paintings of butterflies and other insect pollinators; and text describing the plants, their habitat, and importance to the environment. Countess Clarissa Bonde arranged with Holly Shimizu, Executive Director of the USBG, to host an exhibition of the paintings scheduled to open in February 2014.

Creating this book has been a labor of love of both art and native plants.

October 2013

Bonnie S. Driggers

President
Botanical Artists for Education & the Environment

Virginia Rose
by Margaret Farr

Acknowledgments

Many people contributed to the creation of this book. We were amazed at their enthusiasm and generosity, and we are indebted to all.

Our book is a child of our incorporated nonprofit company, Botanical Artists for Education & the Environment (BAEE). We began as a group of botanical artists in painting classes in Falls Church, Virginia, taught by Anne-Marie Evans, who provided the inspiration for our project. As president, I served as organizer, encourager, fundraiser, and general dogsbody. I relied heavily on our Board of Directors, who worked together to make the project possible.

I doubt there has ever been a more smoothly functioning board: Mary Page Hickey, vice president; Esther Carpi, secretary; Karen Ringstrand, treasurer; Clarissa Bonde, honorary fund-raising chairman; Anne Lewis, judging chairman; Judy Rodgers, publicity chairman; and Mary Elcano, legal consultant.

Keith Tomlinson, Interpretive Naturalist and Manager of Meadowlark Botanical Gardens, encouraged and supported us from the very beginning. He and Nancy Christmus, Conservation Horticulturist and owner of Nativescapes Horticultural Consulting, wrote the initial plant descriptive text. Keith and Nancy are longtime collaborators in native plant horticulture, plant geography of the Potomac River Basin, and interpretation of botanic garden collections to further public understanding of the need to conserve plant diversity in the wild.

The support of Holly Shimizu, Executive Director of the U.S. Botanic Garden, came as a shot in the arm to our project when we had nearly given up. She immediately liked the idea of our book and made suggestions as to its content and, most important, offered to host an exhibition of the paintings. Bill McLaughlin, Plant Curator at the USBG, advised us on content, reviewed the text, suggested several experts that we should consult, and, in general, helped us avoid pitfalls.

In addition, Holly and Bill served on our judging panel along with Dick Rauh, past president of the American Society of Botanical Artists; and Mary Morton, Curator of French Painting at the National Gallery of Art.

Dr. Douglas Tallamy, Professor of Entomology and Wildlife Ecology at the University of Delaware, and author of the book *Bringing Nature Home: How You Can Sustain Wildlife with Native Plants,* wrote the section in the Introduction on the importance of native plants. Dr. Marc Epstein, California Department of Food and Agriculture, reviewed and corrected the section in the Introduction on butterflies and moths. Kyle Wallick, Botanist at the USBG, reviewed and verified botanical information. Marion Lobstein, Professor Emeritus, Northern Virginia Community College, Manassas, who is an expert on mid-Atlantic wildflowers, also reviewed the text.

Old Town Editions, experts in digital printmaking in Alexandria, Virginia, scanned many of the paintings and corrected scans submitted by artists from around the country, this latter gratis and quickly. Dana Sibolt, founder and president of MacMedics, generously lent us Macintosh laptop computers to use for the judging.

After Kim Oster's original fine work on our website, Cynthia Lockley took over, contributed to the final design and layout, and answered web- and Internet-related questions.

Karen Ringstrand, text editor, incorporated information from multiple sources and edited and proofed the entire book. Others contributed by advising, reviewing, and proofreading: Kitty Gilbert, Marsha Ogden, Cynthia Rice, Mary Elcano, Mary Page Hickey, Cynthia Lockley, and Jean Morra.

Our publisher, Lydia Inglett, wonderful in every respect, patiently guided us novices from conception to production to – finally! – the receipt of books.

My special thanks go to my husband, Gerald, who supported the project completely and made sure that I had the time to devote to it.

Bonnie S. Driggers
President, BAEE

Virginia Spiderwort
by Karen Ringstrand

Introduction

Botanical Artists for Education & the Environment (BAEE) created this book, *American Botanical Paintings: Native Plants of the Mid Atlantic,* for lovers of art and plants. We hope to foster a particular appreciation not only for the beauty of native plants and their artistic representations but also for their importance to the environment and to encourage, where practical, the use of native plants in home gardens.

For years, arguments to use more native plants in our gardens have been based more on emotion than on science, but recent research has built a powerful case for increasing the diversity and abundance of natives in our landscapes. Studies have shown that native plants are the backbone around which terrestrial ecosystems are built. Like plants all over the world, native plants turn sunlight into food. That food, however, is useful to consumers only if they can eat it. Because all plants defend their tissues with bitter or toxic chemicals, plant tissues are available only to animals (insects in particular) that have developed the adaptations required to detoxify defensive phytochemicals. Long periods of exposure to a plant lineage are required to develop such adaptations. And this is why replacing native plant communities with non-native plants has been so detrimental to local food webs.

Even though some non-natives have been in North America for hundreds of years, that has not been nearly long enough for local insects to evolve the ability to eat them. Consequently, plants from Asia, Europe, and South America are very poor at supporting insect herbivores. Without insects, most birds cannot reproduce, and freshwater fish as well as spiders, amphibians, lizards, bats, rodents, and many other mammals lose a vital source of protein in their diets. Without insects, animal diversity plummets, ecosystem function decreases, and the ecosystem services that keep humans alive become scarce. We must rebuild our native plant communities not just because we like natives but because we depend on them.

Our book is by no means comprehensive. We selected paintings submitted by artists for a juried competition and did not control their choices except to require that all plants be native to the mid Atlantic. After consulting with Bill McLaughlin, Curator of Plants at the USBG, we defined mid Atlantic somewhat loosely to include the following states: New York, New Jersey, Delaware, Pennsylvania, Maryland, District of Columbia, Virginia, West Virginia, and North Carolina. Within the book's narrow scope, we hope readers find it both beautiful and informative.

We organized alphabetically by common name, for ease of use by a wide variety of readers. We also provided the botanical names for genus, species, and family. An index allows quick searches by genus. Using common instead of botanical names does lead to some problems because many plants go by a variety of common names. We used the United States Department of Agriculture (USDA) Natural Resources Conservation Service (NRCS) Plants Database as our primary authority for botanical and common names, native status and distribution, habitat, and environmental uses. This comprehensive database comprises the native and naturalized plants of the United States and its territories. However, where the USDA database does not reflect the most recent plant family affiliation information, we have followed the Angiosperm Phylogeny Group (APG) III classifications. At times, for consistency, we deviated from the prescribed common family names in the Plants database: for example, using witchhazel instead of witch-hazel. In the case of the two possumhaw plants in the book, we added "viburnum" to the common name for *Viburnum nudum* to distinguish it from the *Ilex decidua,* which also goes by the common name possumhaw.

We included paintings of various insects that are associated with the plants. Butterflies, moths, and bees are all attracted to sweet, delicate scents, but bees, butterflies, and some moths are active during daylight, while other moths visit the night-scented flowers. Flies and beetles may be attracted even by smells that would repel us, for example, the odor of skunk cabbage *(Symplocarpus foetidus)* flowers.

Most insect pollinators are non-discriminating opportunists, feeding wherever they find nectar or other food. There are a number of moths and butterflies that have evolved an association with particular plants, such as the Monarch butterfly with milkweeds. Although the adult Monarchs are non-discriminating pollinators, they frequent milkweed for nectar, and their larvae prefer eating the milkweed leaves. These plants contain a poisonous substance that is stored in the bodies of both caterpillars and adult butterflies, thus providing a defense against predators. In another curious relationship, Yucca Moth caterpillars eat only yucca seeds and only Yucca Moths pollinate the plant. We mentioned similar associations where appropriate.

For each plant painting, we briefly described the plants and their habitats, provided relevant information about the plant families, and related ways in which Native Americans or early settlers used the plants. For plants unsuitable for home gardens, we mentioned their environmental importance, such as food and habitat for birds and animals.

We hope you enjoy the beautiful paintings and find their stories useful and entertaining.

Dense Blazing Star
by Sara Joline Bedford

Adam's Needle

Yucca filamentosa
Asparagaceae (Asparagus Family)

Found growing in fields and on roadsides, beaches, and sand dunes, Adam's needle thrives in full sun. The rosette of stiff bayonet-like leaves lasts throughout the year. The leaf margins are marked by delicate curling filaments, giving the species its name. In May a central stalk emerges from the rosette of leaves and produces a large cluster of cream to white flowers that bloom in June and July. The flowers are large, waxy, and bell-shaped.

Formerly in the agave family, Adam's needle is now classified as part of the asparagus family. Native to the southeastern United States, west to Louisiana and north to Virginia, the plant is sometimes found even farther north into New England. Native Americans used an infusion of Adam's needle to treat diabetes and sores. They used the root for soap and the fibrous leaves for making mats. The flowers and fruit may be eaten. The only known pollinator for *Yucca filamentosa* is the Yucca Moth *(Tegeticula yuccasella)* shown below. The plant and insect are interdependent: the moth's larvae require the seeds of the yucca plant, and the plant can be pollinated only by the Yucca Moth.

Adam's needle is grown in home gardens and public garden collections. Given time it will spread and form a handsome group of plants. Sandy, acid soils are preferred whether on a mountain slope or coastal dune.

The small and inconspicuous Yucca Moth *(Tegeticula yuccasella)* has a wingspan of only $^{11}/_{16}$ to 1½ inches. Painting by Kandy Phillips.

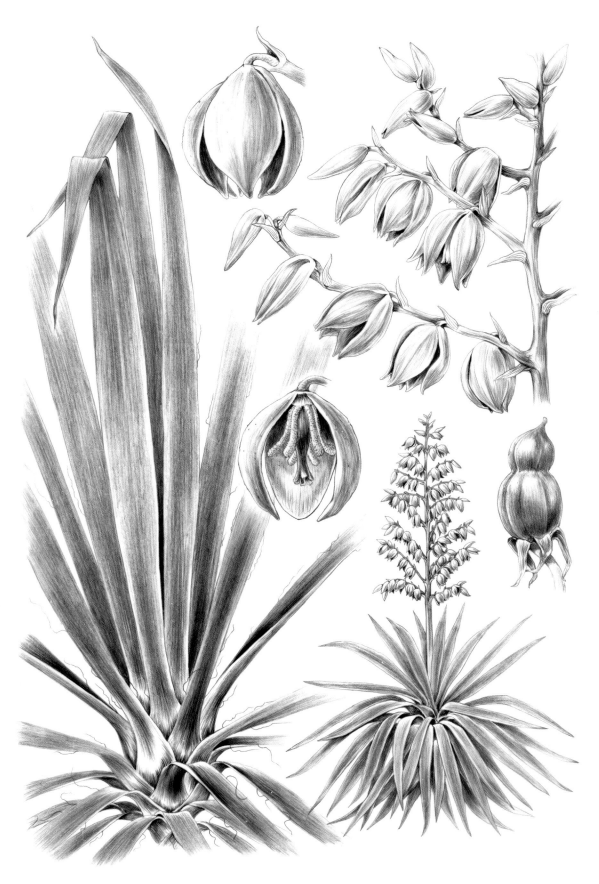

Adam's Needle by Alice Tangerini

American Beautyberry by Karen Coleman

American Beautyberry

Callicarpa americana
Lamiaceae (Mint Family)

With its clusters of brilliant magenta fruits, the American beautyberry is a popular ornamental shrub now cultivated in many parts of the temperate world. This deciduous perennial with its graceful arching branches usually grows from 3 to 5 feet tall, but under favorable conditions may grow to 9 feet. Small pink flowers appear in spring, but the real attraction comes in fall as the dramatic fruit clusters mature and hug the stem at the leaf axils. The berries persist into midwinter after the leaves have fallen. Found from Maryland to Texas in an arc across the southeast, beautyberry also appears in some inland Appalachian highland habitats.

The mint family has a wide distribution and includes quite a few familiar herbs such as basil, mint, and rosemary, as well as some shrubs and trees, such as teak. Altogether there are more than 7,000 species. Many birds, particularly the Northern Bobwhite, enjoy beautyberry fruit. Native Americans used the roots and leaves for various medicinal purposes, including treating malarial fevers. American beautyberry contains the chemical callicarpenal that has been patented by the USDA Agricultural Research Service as a mosquito repellent.

A superb specimen shrub or border plant, beautyberry grows easily in a variety of soils in full sun to partial shade.

The Common Buckeye butterfly (*Junonia coenia*), with a wingspan of 1⅝ to 2¾ inches, will gather nectar from a variety of plants, including beautyberry. Painting by Kandy Phillips.

American Witchhazel by Chiara Becchi

American Witchhazel

Hamamelis virginiana
Hamamelidaceae (Witchhazel Family)

In autumn, the delicate, fragrant blossoms of the witchhazel appear, with their unusual long, slender, curly petals. The yellow blooms persist after the leaves have fallen. Hard brown seed capsules last through winter and ripen the following spring. When the seeds pop out of the capsule, they can travel as far as 30 feet. In the painting the left branch shows the seed capsules and leaves as they appear in the summer. The branch on the right is in flower, with autumn foliage. An excellent understory plant, this native is found in deciduous forests throughout the eastern United States and as far west as Texas.

Birds eat the fruit and seeds. Witchhazel extract, a mild astringent, is distilled from the twigs and bark. Native Americans used the shrub for a multitude of ailments, including aching muscles, cuts, and insect bites. The Cherokee made a tea from the leaves and twigs. Forked witchhazel branches were used as divining rods for dowsing, to locate groundwater or buried treasure.

This versatile and adaptable plant can be used as a multistemmed shrub or pruned up to a small tree, usually 10 to 15 feet tall. It tolerates shade and prefers moist conditions.

Azure Bluet

Houstonia caerulea
Rubiaceae (Madder Family)

In late spring, the delicate blue flowers of azure bluet appear in lawns and open woodlands. Growing in small tufts to approximately 4 inches in height, these tiny native flowers have four light blue petals with a bright yellow center. Given the right conditions, there will be hundreds of plants blanketing the ground. Azure bluets are found in open fields and along stream banks up and down the East Coast as far north as Canada and south to Louisiana.

Pollinators love these little flowers for their nectar and pollen. Azure bluets are also known as "Quaker Ladies," so called because the blue color was said to resemble the color of a Quaker lady's dress and the shape of the flower, her hat. In the madder family, azure bluets are related to coffee, quinine, buttonbush, and gardenia.

Besides azure bluets, the painting illustrates marsh blue violet *(Viola cucullata* var. *sororia)*, maple *(Acer)*, and Small Cabbage White butterflies *(Pieris rapae)*, which have a wingspan of 1¾ to 2¼ inches. These butterflies gather nectar from a variety of plants including mustards, dandelions, red clover, asters, and mints. Accidentally introduced to the United States, this insect causes considerable damage to commercial crops in the cabbage family.

Azure bluets tolerate a range of soil from acidic rocky outcrops to alkaline grassy areas; although they prefer sun, they will easily grow in a semi-shady area. Growing bluets in the garden can be tricky: they seem to require a patch of moss and sunlight to settle in happily. They can be grown in lawns, but care must be taken not to mow until they have set seed.

Azure Bluet with Marsh Blue Violet, Maple, and Small Cabbage White Butterflies
by Margaret Farr

Birdfoot Violet by Karen Coleman

Birdfoot Violet

Viola pedata
Violaceae (Violet Family)

Often considered the most beautiful species of the violet family, birdfoot violets display some variety in coloration. The most dramatic is the bicolored flower with two velvety, deep purple petals on top and three contrasting light blue or lavender lower petals (shown in the painting). Solid color blooms range from lavender to blue, all with brilliant orange anthers on the five stamens. The violet reaches heights of 4 to 10 inches and stands out from other natives not only for its color but also for its deeply lobed leaves resembling a bird's foot.

Violaceae contain over 800 species, including trees and shrubs. At least 80 of the species are violets inhabiting the United States and Canada. The sweet-smelling *Viola odorata* is a European member of this group famously used in perfumes. Birdfoot violet serves as the larval host for the increasingly rare Regal Fritillary butterfly (*Speyeria idalia*), shown here.

This violet grows from the East Coast to the Great Plains in dry, sunny, upland sites. Birdfoot violet is one of the more challenging violets to grow in the garden, as it prefers a sandy soil and requires excellent drainage.

The Regal Fritillary butterfly (*Speyeria idalia*) has an average wingspan of approximately 1 to 4 inches. Shown also is its mature larva. Paintings by Karen Ringstrand.

Black Walnut

Juglans nigra
Juglandaceae (Walnut Family)

In spring the compound leaves of the black walnut appear, measuring up to 2 feet in length and comprising leaflets along a main rib. A tough, leathery, yellow-green hull encases the nut; in autumn the hull turns black, and the nut falls from the tree. The walnut tree can reach heights of 100 feet and more.

The walnut family has only 60 species, mostly trees, with 21 species native to the United States, including walnut, hickory, and pecan. The economic importance of the black walnut is astonishing: its wood is used to make furniture and rifle stocks; the high-protein nuts, more strongly flavored than English walnuts, are edible; and the outer hull of the nut, when finely crushed, is used as an abrasive. The tannins that turn the outer hull of the walnut black have been used as a dye for millennia. Not surprisingly, Native Americans had many traditional uses for the black walnut, not only as food, but also for carving, dyes, and medicine. Black walnut is the preferred larval host for both the Luna (*Actias luna*) and Royal Walnut (*Citheronia regalis*) moths (see below).

The black walnut is a magnificent specimen tree. A sunny location and rich, fertile soil are required for this tree to thrive. The black walnut exudes from its roots a chemical called juglone that prevents the nearby growth of many other native species of plants, including columbine, chokeberry, and blueberries.

Shown here are the Royal Walnut moth (*Citheronia regalis*), with a wingspan of 3$\frac{5}{16}$ to 6¼ inches, and its fearsome-looking, but harmless, caterpillar, the Hickory Horned Devil. Paintings by Kandy Phillips.

Black Walnut by Jessica Tcherepnine

Blackeyed Susan by Esther Carpi

Blackeyed Susan

Rudbeckia hirta
Asteraceae (Aster Family)

Blackeyed Susan is a daisy-like flower that blooms in the summer and early fall throughout the United States. The bloom, which is 2 to 3 inches across, is composed of bright yellow rays surrounding the dark brown center that contains the flower parts. The plant, which has hairy leaves and stems, grows up to 2 feet tall.

The aster family comprises over 20 species of *Rudbeckia*, all native to North America. They range in height from 2 to 10 feet. Found worldwide, the large family includes chrysanthemums and zinnias. Native Americans used the roots of blackeyed Susan to treat colds, earaches, and snakebites. The flowers are a good nectar source for bees, butterflies, and insects. The plant is the larval host for the Bordered Patch (*Chlosyne lacinia*), the Gorgone Checkerspot (*Chlosyne gorgone*), and the Silvery Checkerspot (*Chlosyne nycteis*) butterflies, the latter of which is shown here. Birds eat the seeds.

Growing in fields and along roadsides, blackeyed Susans prefer dry soil and sunny areas. Though the plant is actually a biennial, it is often considered a perennial since it easily reseeds itself. Extensive breeding programs have produced many attractive cultivars including the ever-popular 'Toto' and 'Indian Summer.'

Blackeyed Susans serve as larval host plants for the Silvery Checkerspot butterfly (*Chlosyne nycteis*); its wingspan is $1\frac{3}{8}$ to 2 inches. Painting by Kandy Phillips.

Blue Wild Indigo by Jerry Kurtzweg

Blue Wild Indigo

Baptisia australis
Fabaceae (Pea Family)

From mid May to early June, blue wild indigo produces lovely blue or purple blooms. The flower shape is typical for the pea family. This plant can become quite large for a wildflower, sometimes reaching 4 feet in height. The bloom is followed by a classic gray to black bean pod; the seeds, which have hard coats, are prolific.

The pea family includes large equatorial trees, arctic herbs, and desert shrubs. Three distinct subfamilies account for some 700 genera and 17,000 species. Redbud is among many popular ornamental plants in the family. Perhaps the most important members of the pea family are the food crops, such as beans, peas, peanuts, and soybeans. Native Americans used blue wild indigo for medicinal purposes as well as for blue dye. Early European settlers also used the plant to create a blue dye, which was an inferior substitute for true indigo. Blue wild indigo is valuable ecologically for attracting native bees.

This is a superb plant as a specimen or in groupings. While the bloom time is short, the foliage and seedpods keep blue wild indigo visually interesting throughout the growing season. As with many members of Fabaceae, the roots "fix" nitrogen and enrich soils. While blue wild indigo will flourish in rich soils, it also does well in less desirable locations. Seeds are easily collected for further plantings but these will take a few seasons to mature. Full sun is needed for good flowering.

Shown here, the female Clouded Sulphur butterfly (*Colias philodice*) uses plants in the pea family as caterpillar hosts. The wingspan is 2½ to 2¾ inches. Painting by Kandy Phillips.

Broadleaf Cattail
by Jessica Tcherepnine

Broadleaf Cattail

Typha latifolia
Typhaceae (Cattail Family)

As common as it is graceful, broadleaf cattail is often coveted by wetland naturalists and largely overlooked by gardeners. Its long lance-like leaves and unique columnar flower are recognized by anyone who frequents freshwater lakes and rivers. The painting shows the cylindrical flowering spike on the right side. Later in the season the spike disintegrates, forming the fluffy "tail" seen on the left. Once winter arrives, the entire plant dies back, leaving tawny leaves at the water's edge.

The cattail family has just one genus and fifteen species worldwide. A wetland plant, broadleaf cattail carries out several important ecological functions. It attracts numerous marsh birds seeking cover from predators. At the same time, it conceals fish and frogs from larger wading birds hunting about its margins. The prolific foliage shelters fish eggs, frog eggs, and numerous aquatic insects. In addition, cattails can filter and catch sediment in urbanized storm-water ponds.

Native Americans used many parts of the plant, including the starchy roots that they collected and cooked. The young flower head can be eaten when boiled, and newly emerged foliage provides asparagus-like greens. Leaves are collected to make mats and baskets.

Though aggressive, cattails are useful and ornamental plants in water gardens or along pond margins, and can be grown in containers.

Canadian Wildginger

Asarum canadense
Aristolochiaceae (Birthwort Family)

Few native plants display such lush, velvety foliage as Canadian wildginger. The heart-shaped leaves are nearly luminescent on the forest floor when they appear in mid spring. Shortly afterward the single reddish-brown flowers appear at ground level where they are often hidden by the leaves. The corolla is entirely fused, but three distinct petals take shape at the margin. The roots are aromatic when crushed, resembling culinary ginger.

The birthwort family has seven genera and four hundred species, often vines with large, ornate tubular flowers. While primarily a tropical group, a few are native to eastern North America, including Dutchman's pipe. Native Americans used Canadian wildginger roots, which have been found to have antibiotic properties, to make a poultice for wounds. But, as with many plants, there are some mildly toxic parts.

Asarum canadense is a common groundcover in mid-Atlantic forests. Growing to approximately 6 inches in height, it will slowly spread to fill an area. Easy to grow and widely available commercially, wildginger is highly recommended for the woodland garden. This plant contains a bitter-tasting substance, aristolochic acid, that discourages predators, making it a successful groundcover where deer are present.

Canadian Wildginger by Lara Call Gastinger

Cardinalflower by Annie Patterson

Cardinalflower

Lobelia cardinalis
Campanulaceae (Bellflower Family)

Reaching heights of 5 feet, the cardinalflower produces a spire of vivid scarlet flowers in midsummer. The tubular blossoms start opening at the bottom of the raceme and offer a lingering floral display. Cardinalflower thrives in moist areas, along stream banks and wetlands in most of the continental United States. The plant was imported to Europe in the seventeenth century, and it is there that the common name, said to derive from the color of a cardinal's robe, originated.

The bellflower family is primarily herbaceous with a few shrubs, all containing a milky sap. Native Americans used the roots and leaves of cardinalflower to treat a variety of ailments, including headaches and worms. Hummingbirds, including the Ruby-throated Hummingbird (*Archilochus colubris*) shown here, are the primary pollinators for the cardinalflower due to the long tubular shape of its flowers.

This perennial is a wonderful addition to the garden, offering brilliant red color in summer. Cardinalflower generously reseeds in ideal conditions, where there is constant moisture in the soil. The plant contains a naturally occurring alkaloid, lobeline, which discourages herbivores from browsing. The substance is also used to treat drug addiction. Cultivars and hybrids have blooms of white, pink, and purple, in addition to red.

The Ruby-throated Hummingbird (*Archilochus colubris*) is a primary pollinator for cardinalflower. Painting by Kandy Phillips.

Cinnamon Fern

Osmunda cinnamomea
Osmundaceae (Royal Fern Family)

In early spring, silvery green fiddleheads unfurl to release the majestic green foliage of the cinnamon fern. First to appear are the erect fertile fronds that are initially green but become cinnamon colored. The infertile fronds bend outward and are longer.

The ancient royal fern family is small with about 20 species. Fossilized records of *Osmunda cinnamomea* have been found dating back 70 million years. Other ferns from this prehistoric family in the mid-Atlantic flora are the royal fern and the interrupted fern. Root fibers of the cinnamon fern are harvested commercially for use in potting orchids and other epiphytes.

Found throughout the eastern United States and as far west as Texas and Oklahoma and north to Missouri, Iowa, and Minnesota, cinnamon ferns inhabit bogs and moist areas of the forest, preferring wet soil and partially shady areas. Usually 3 feet tall and wide, they can reach heights of 5 feet given satisfactory conditions. Cinnamon ferns can be successfully grown in full sun given proper moisture. They make a dramatic addition to the garden with their contrasting fronds.

Cinnamon Fern by Judith C. Towers

Common Persimmon by Bonnie S. Driggers

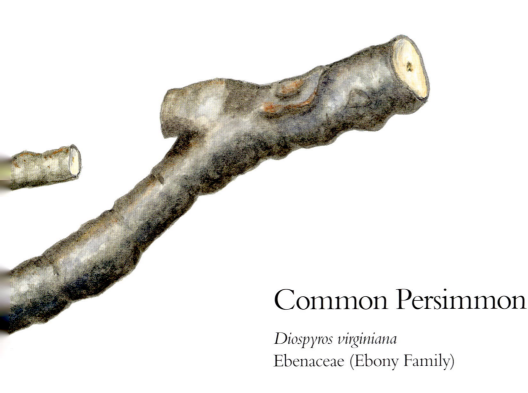

Common Persimmon

Diospyros virginiana
Ebenaceae (Ebony Family)

Common persimmon is a deciduous tree that grows from 30 to 80 feet tall, and has small, nodding flowers with a yellowish corolla. The tree produces small, fleshy orange fruit that when ripe is sweet and delicious and can be eaten raw or baked into puddings and cakes. However, the immature fruit is extremely astringent. On older trees the distinctive bark is very dark colored and thick with deep fissures.

One of only two genera in the ebony family, *Diospyros* is the more complex, accounting for nearly 500 species that are largely tropical. In the tropics this genus provides the valuable black "African ebony" wood. Other *Diospyros* species are widely cultivated in Asia for their fruit. An important fall forage fruit for Woodland Indians of eastern North America, common persimmon served as a remedy for sore throat and toothache. Native Americans used the extremely hard wood for carving, and it is still used for billiard cues and shoe lasts. Long used for heads of golf clubs, persimmon is still preferred by some golfers over the newer metal heads. Many mammals and birds feed on the fruit. Common persimmon is a larval host for the Luna moth (*Actias luna*), and is a good nectar source for honeybees.

Common persimmon is a valuable addition to the garden as an understory or accent tree. Two trees are needed to produce fruit.

Common Winterberry

Ilex verticillata
Aquifoliaceae (Holly Family)

Valued for its dramatic red fruit, the common winterberry is a member of the holly family. Inconspicuous white flowers appear in late spring, followed by the berries. This holly is not evergreen; the dark green leaves, which are not as sharply pointed as those of other hollies, turn a light purplish color in fall and drop off. The red berries remain throughout the winter, making this a very attractive addition to the garden. The light gray bark also provides winter interest.

The holly family comprises woody plants that generally prefer acidic soils. A popular tea, Yerba Maté, is produced from the leaves of a South American species. Squirrels and birds, including robins, eat the fruit of the common winterberry. Native Americans made a tea from the bark to reduce fevers.

Reaching heights of 6 to 10 feet, and even taller under ideal conditions, this adaptable shrub can handle shade or sun, but prefers moist soil. A gardener will need to plant both male and female shrubs to ensure fruiting.

Common Winterberry by Margaret Farr

Crimsoneyed Rosemallow by Marcia Long

Crimsoneyed Rosemallow

Hibiscus moscheutos
Malvaceae (Mallow Family)

The showy, exotic-looking crimsoneyed rosemallow blooms in the summer along rivers and wetlands of the mid Atlantic. Flower colors vary from white to red, and dark crimson centers contrast with the yellow anthers and stigma. The five petals are delicate and tissue-like, while the leaves are large and heart-shaped.

Malvaceae contain a few economically important plants, such as cotton, okra, and cacao beans used to make chocolate. Crimsoneyed rosemallow attracts many pollinators, including hummingbirds.

This attractive plant is easily grown from seed and does well in a garden, preferring full sun with moist soil conditions. It will quickly grow to 6 to 8 feet. Because this perennial is late to emerge in the spring, gardeners should mark its location if the old stalks have been removed.

The Painted Lady butterfly (*Vanessa cardui*) obtains nectar from many flowers, including mallows. Its wingspan is 2 to $2^{7}/_{8}$ inches. Painting by Kandy Phillips.

Crossvine

Bignonia capreolata
Bignoniaceae (Trumpet-creeper Family)

Crossvine is a handsome vine covered in showy blossoms in late spring and sporadically throughout the summer. The 2-inch-long tubular flowers grow in clusters. They may be all vermilion, vermilion with yellow centers, or yellow with red centers. The leaves are green and glossy in the summer and provide winter interest with a coppery hue. A cross section of the stem shows the distinct segments of the water and food transportation systems, giving this vine its common name. Always searching for the sunlight, crossvine is found scrambling up trees and growing alongside streams in a natural setting. It can grow up to 50 feet long.

The trumpet-creeper family is primarily tropical but has a few other representatives in the mid Atlantic, including the *Catalpa* tree. Native Americans used an infusion of the crossvine leaves to treat rheumatism. The flowers attract hummingbirds, butterflies, and other pollinators; even raccoons have been known to eat them.

Crossvine is a versatile and fast-growing semi-evergreen plant that tolerates full sun to full shade; however, it blooms only infrequently in the shade. This vine makes an outstanding screen or living fence. Crossvine prefers the acidic moist soils of the Piedmont. 'Dragon Lady' and 'Tangerine' are popular cultivars selected for their rich colors.

Crossvine by Cynthia Rice

Curlyheads Seed Head by Pamela Mason

Curlyheads

Clematis ochroleuca
Ranunculaceae (Buttercup Family)

Found on roadsides and in open woodlands, curlyheads are highly distinctive in flower and fruit. In spring the solitary nodding flower is poised at the top of an arching stem. The flower is thick and leathery with reflexed petals. Pale yellow to pale purple in color, it is covered in short silvery hairs. The nearly stemless opposite leaves give the entire plant a neat upright architecture. In fall the seed head (shown in the drawing) forms a curious feathery, spider-like structure. Absent almost entirely from the coastal plain and Appalachians, curlyheads are denizens of the rolling Piedmont from Virginia into the Carolinas and west to Tennessee.

A member of the buttercup family, *Clematis* is a widespread genus in tropical and temperate regions. There are few woody members of the buttercup family, which also includes the poisonous native, monkshood.

Curlyheads are available from specialty native plant growers in the mid Atlantic. Reaching 1 to 2 feet in height, a clump of curlyheads is beautiful and intriguing. Curlyheads tolerate full sun or partial shade.

Dense Blazing Star

Liatris spicata
Asteraceae (Aster Family)

In late spring, the first sign of dense blazing star appears as a tuft of grass-like green leaves. By midsummer, the stalk grows 3 to 4 feet and releases feathery rosy-purple flowers that bloom from the top to the bottom. The painting shows the delicate individual blooms enlarged. This species is normally found growing in slightly moist conditions in the eastern half of the United States and Canada.

An ornamental member of Asteraceae, the genus includes roughly 40 species, most native to North America. Native Americans used the root of dense blazing star to treat colic and other ailments. The long-lasting flowers attract butterflies, bumblebees, and hummingbirds. In autumn when the flowers go to seed, they provide nourishment for birds, such as goldfinches.

Dense blazing star grows in sun or partial shade. Sometimes called florist gayfeather, *Liatris spicata* is popular for floral arrangements.

The Wavy-lined Emerald moth (*Synchlora aerata*), with a wingspan of about $^{11}/_{16}$ of an inch, obtains nectar from a variety of plants, including species of *Liatris*. Its unusual caterpillar, the Camouflaged Looper, attaches tiny bits of plants on its back to confuse predators. Paintings by Kandy Phillips.

Dense Blazing Star by Sara Joline Bedford

Downy Rattlesnake Plantain by Lee Boulay D'Zmura

Downy Rattlesnake Plantain

Goodyera pubescens
Orchidaceae (Orchid Family)

Dark green, white-etched leaves resembling a snake's skin give this native gem its common name. The attractive leaves form a rosette from which the 6- to 18-inch flower stalk grows, producing an inflorescence of tiny white orchids in midsummer.

Downy rattlesnake plantain is a member of Orchidaceae, one of the largest plant families, containing over 20,000 species. Worldwide in distribution, they are often endangered by habitat degradation and over-collection. Vanilla is a well-known member of the family. In the tropics most orchids are epiphytes, growing on tree trunks and crowns. In cooler temperate ecosystems, they are all terrestrial. Native Americans used the roots of downy rattlesnake plantain to treat snakebites as well as other ailments, including pleurisy.

This delightful little orchid appears in woodlands clustered in groups. It is relatively easy to grow and does well in the garden when planted in partial shade in slightly acidic soil.

Dwarf Witchalder

Fothergilla gardenii
Hamamelidaceae (Witchhazel Family)

Compact clusters of fragrant white flowers appear in terminal spikes on this lovely shrub in spring. The bottlebrush-like blooms feature prominent white stamens with yellowish anthers. The dark green, leathery leaves appear after the blooms and offer summer interest with their well-defined venation. The leaves turn yellow, orange, or red in the fall.

Only five species of the witchhazel family are native to the United States; these include American witchhazel and sweetgum. *Fothergilla gardenii* was named after John Fothergill, an English physician and plantsman who introduced many American natives to Europe.

Native to the southeastern United States, from North Carolina to Alabama, dwarf witchalder is an attractive addition to the garden, with its fragrant blooms in spring and bright color in fall. It deserves to be more widely planted. It grows well when grouped with rhododendrons, preferring the same moist acidic soils.

Dwarf Witchalder by Chiara Becchi

Eastern Leatherwood by Alice Tangerini

Eastern Leatherwood

Dirca palustris
Thymelaeaceae (Mezereum Family)

Eastern leatherwood is perhaps the earliest flowering shrub in the mid-Atlantic forest. The yellow, tubular flowers are only ½ to ¾ inch long. Dark green leaves do not emerge entirely until after the blooms are gone. A trademark shrub of eastern deciduous woodlands, leatherwood has a surprisingly large range, reaching across the Mississippi Basin, south to Florida, and north to the Canadian Maritimes.

The mezereum family is a largely tropical group with some temperate outliers. Several noteworthy shrubs in the family are widely cultivated, especially those in the genus *Daphne*. Native Americans used the bark and twigs of eastern leatherwood for twine. They used decoctions of the bark and root as laxatives, analgesics, and hair washes. Many parts of the plant are toxic.

Although not widely available commercially, eastern leatherwood makes a good addition to the shady or partly shady garden.

Eastern Purple Coneflower

Echinacea purpurea
Asteraceae (Aster Family)

Lavender-pink, drooping rays encircle the spiny, cone-shaped center of the eastern purple coneflower. Growing to 2 to 3 feet in height, with rough, dark green leaves, the coneflower blooms throughout the summer. The distinctive cones, which give the plant its common name, persist into winter.

There are nearly 20,000 species in the large aster family, many of which are drought tolerant and well adapted to urban settings. Sunflowers, dandelions, and marigolds are other family members. Eastern purple coneflowers are popular with pollinators, including butterflies and hummingbirds, and are valuable to native bees. Birds, especially goldfinches, enjoy the seed heads in the fall. Native Americans chewed the roots as a treatment for dyspepsia and cough. European colonists were quick to follow the natives' example by using the flowers to make an herbal tea to strengthen the immune system.

Echinacea purpurea is a very popular garden perennial, with colors of the flower ranging from white to purple to shades of red. It is easy to grow in partial shade to full sun.

Eastern Purple Coneflower with Eastern Tiger Swallowtail by Karen Ringstrand

Eastern Redbud by Juliet Kirby

Eastern Redbud

Cercis canadensis
Fabaceae (Pea Family)

The small purple flowers emerge directly from branches and occasionally from the trunk of the eastern redbud in spring, before the leaves appear. This showy native brightens the spring forest as well as many gardens in the mid Atlantic. The attractive leaves are heart-shaped. Rarely more than 20 feet high, the redbud has a graceful, spreading habit.

The pea family comprises a variety of plants from trees to herbs, many with bacterial nodules in the roots to fix nitrogen for plant use. Chickpeas, clover, and wisteria are members of this important taxonomic group. Native Americans ate redbud flowers and used an infusion of the roots and bark to treat fever and whooping cough. Redbud flowers are an important nectar source for bees, butterflies, moths, and other insects; the tree provides good nesting sites for birds; and seeds from the tree provide winter food for birds and squirrels.

Redbud is at home in full sun or shade. The pea pod capsules are abundant in late summer and fall. There are many cultivars, such as the purple-leaved 'Forest Pansy.'

Cercis canadensis is one of several plants, including some hollies, blueberries, and viburnums, that serve as caterpillar hosts for the Henry's Elfin butterfly (*Callophrys henrici*). The wingspan is only 1 to 1¼ inches. Painting by Kandy Phillips.

Flame Azalea

Rhododendron calendulaceum
Ericaceae (Heath Family)

This spectacular native shrub of the Appalachian Mountains steals the show with fiery blossoms in the late spring to early summer. The clusters of tubular flowers, larger than those of other *Rhododendron* species, can vary in color from yellow to orange or red. The flowers generally appear before the leaves.

In addition to the genus *Rhododendron*, the heath family also includes heather, blueberry, and wintergreen. Like most members of Ericaceae, flame azalea prefers acidic soil. Native Americans rubbed boiled twigs on rheumatic joints, and the Cherokee used the flowers to decorate their homes. All parts of the plant are toxic.

This native shrub, which can grow up to 12 feet tall, prefers some sunlight for best flowering and tolerates dry soil. A lovely addition to mid-Atlantic gardens due to its showy spring display, flame azalea is attractive to butterflies and bees.

The adult Pipevine Swallowtail butterfly (*Battus philenor*), which has a wingspan of 2¾ to 5 inches, gathers nectar from a variety of flowers, including rhododendrons. Host plants for their caterpillars are various *Aristolochia* spp. Painting by Kandy Phillips.

Flame Azalea by Holly Maillet

Flowering Dogwood

Cornus florida
Cornaceae (Dogwood Family)

Flowering dogwood is one of the loveliest small native flowering trees, particularly in late spring when its bright white flowers appear in eastern woodlands. The four white "petals" of the blossoms are actually large bracts, which surround the inner cluster of small yellow flowers. Red fruit and fall foliage follow the spectacular spring bloom. Even in winter the dogwood provides visual interest with its graceful shape and distinctive bark. The blossoms of the native species are generally white, but there are many cultivars with pink and red blooms. Reaching 20 to 40 feet in height, this deciduous tree ranges along the Eastern Seaboard west to the Mississippi River Basin.

The fruit provides food for birds and mammals, and the plant serves as the larval host for both the Spring Azure butterfly (*Celastrina ladon*) and the Cecropia Silkmoth *(Hyalophora cecropia)* shown here. Native Americans used the root and bark to treat fevers and malaria and to produce a red dye. They used the wood for carving and making loom shuttles.

An ideal small native tree for the garden, the dogwood is at home in partial shade and full sun with proper moisture. In summer, the flowering dogwood frequently suffers from anthracnose leaf fungus that causes brown patches on leaves and twig dieback. 'Appalachian Spring' is a selection with natural resistance to this fungus.

The Cecropia Silkmoth *(Hyalophora cecropia)* has a wingspan of $4\frac{5}{16}$ to $5\frac{7}{8}$ inches. Painting by Kandy Phillips.

Flowering Dogwood by Ingrid Arnesen

Greek Valerian by Sara Joline Bedford

Greek Valerian

Polemonium reptans
Polemoniaceae (Phlox Family)

In late spring, clusters of tiny chicory-blue flowers of Greek valerian bloom in deciduous forests of the mid Atlantic. Small native pollinators flit around the bell-shaped flowers, which are only ½ inch in size with five petals and a prominent stigma and anthers. The bright green compound leaves persist through summer and send out the occasional flower if conditions are moist and cool.

A small family mostly found in North America, Polemoniaceae include such important garden plants as the genera *Phlox* and *Ipomopsis*. Greek valerian is valuable for native bees and bumblebees, such as the one (*Bombus* spp.) shown here. According to folklore, *Polemonium reptans*, also known as Jacob's ladder, was so-called for the alternating arrangement of the leaflets on the stem resembling the ladder to heaven the biblical Jacob saw in his dreams.

Preferring partial shade but tolerating more sun with proper moisture, it inhabits the deciduous forests in the mid Atlantic and may be found along streambeds. It is available commercially and would be an attractive addition to a shady garden.

Bumblebees, such as the *Bombus* spp., feed on the tiny flowers of Greek valerian. Painting by Kandy Phillips.

Highbush Blueberry

Vaccinium corymbosum
Ericaceae (Heath Family)

Native to the eastern half of the United States and Canada, highbush blueberry is the parent of cultivated blueberries. Clusters of bell-shaped, pink or white flowers bloom in late springtime, followed by the familiar fruit. The multi-stemmed highbush blueberry has brilliant red foliage in the fall. This deciduous shrub grows in partial shade to sun and prefers acidic soils.

Almost 20 native species of *Vaccinium* are known in North America. The fruit of the highbush blueberry is a valuable food source for bears, other mammals, and many birds. Various pollinators, including butterflies, such as the Spring Azures (*Celastrina ladon*) shown here, are attracted to the flowers. The leaves serve as a host plant for some caterpillars. High in antioxidants, the berries were dried and eaten year round by some tribes of Native Americans, who called the preserved berries "sautaash."

Highbush blueberry grows to 6 to 8 feet. With its fruit and autumn foliage, it makes a delightful addition to a garden.

The Spring Azure butterfly (*Celastrina ladon*) has a wingspan of ⅞ to 1⅜ inches. The larger here is the female. Paintings by Kandy Phillips.

Highbush Blueberry by Sara Joline Bedford

Kentucky Lady's Slipper by Tomoko Connolly

Kentucky Lady's Slipper

Cypripedium kentuckiense
Orchidaceae (Orchid Family)

The Kentucky lady's slipper, which grows up to 2 feet in height, has the largest flower of the *Cypripedium* genus. Its creamy yellow pouch is suspended beneath the purple and green streaked petals and sepals. Single leaves alternate on the erect stem. Kentucky lady's slipper prefers a partially shaded area and tolerates a range of soils from alluvial deposits to sandy slopes. This species of terrestrial orchid is rare in the mid Atlantic, with a few natural colonies existing in Virginia. Most of the populations of *Cypripedium kentuckiense* reside farther west and south in states such as Kentucky, Georgia, and Arkansas.

Part of the orchid family, the lady's slippers make up a distinct sub-family notable for their unique bulbous flowers. Like other terrestrial orchids, the lady's slippers have a complex relationship with fungi in the soil and are best conserved in the wild.

A recent cooperative effort between the Kisatchie National Forest of Louisiana and the Central Louisiana Orchid Society (CLOS) is underway to restore this native orchid. The plants are also being successfully propagated by seed *in vitro*. The Kentucky lady's slipper may be cultivated in dappled shade in slightly acid garden soils.

Lizard's Tail

Saururus cernuus
Saururaceae (Lizard's Tail Family)

White, slender racemes adorn lizard's tail in summer. Fragrant and long-blooming flowers coupled with heart-shaped leaves make this wetland species stand out among the cattails. *Saururus cernuus* is present along the East Coast of the United States and across the Mississippi River west to Oklahoma. The common name, lizard's tail, derives from the botanical genus name, *Saururus*. The Greek word "sauros" means lizard. The species name, *cernuus*, derives from the Latin word for "nodding," which refers to the flower's habit.

Saururaceae contain only seven species of aromatic plants. Native Americans used the roots of lizard's tail to create a poultice to treat injuries. In addition to providing cover, the leaves are a food source for ducks and beavers. Turtles also eat their leaves and bees and butterflies enjoy their nectar.

Lizard's tail colonizes fresh and brackish ponds and streams. It can tolerate full sun to shade; however, it does require moisture to survive. It is best grown in a wetland setting or in a container where it can be kept moist.

Lizard's Tail by Annie Patterson

Moccasin Flower by Judy Rodgers

Moccasin Flower

Cypripedium acaule
Orchidaceae (Orchid Family)

The moccasin flower is perhaps the best-known lady's slipper orchid in the mid Atlantic. Frequently found in pine forests, this orchid is also at home in older oak-hickory woodlands. The Shenandoah and Great Smoky Mountains National Parks host populations of this exquisite plant. The moccasin flower is unmistakable with its red-veined pink "pouch," which has evolved to invite pollinators. The leaves are large with deep parallel venation. Native Americans used the roots for medicinal purposes, including treatment of kidney and urinary tract disorders.

Unavailable commercially, moccasin flowers are highly sensitive to soil disruption. As a result, they must be wholly conserved in the wild. Even in an ideal situation, they require just the right soil conditions to persist and thrive. When ongoing forest succession changes growing conditions, entire wild colonies may vanish. All lady's slipper orchids need protection from collection in the wild and potential theft in public garden collections.

Mountain Laurel

Kalmia latifolia
Ericaceae (Heath Family)

This magnificent broadleaf evergreen shrub displays clusters of stunning bell-shaped pink or white flowers in late May to early June. The new leaves are bright yellow-green and become darker green and leathery later in the season. The shrub is long limbed and open in full shade and compact when more sun is available. This widespread native lives in the eastern half of the United States, where its natural habitat varies from mountainous slopes to bogs and cove forests of the Appalachian Mountains.

Dense thickets of mountain laurel provide protection for songbirds and small mammals. The plant serves as a larval host for the Laurel Sphinx moth (*Sphinx kalmiae*). Native Americans used the wood to make spoons and trowels: hence one of the many common names, spoonwood. They also used the leaves to produce an analgesic and disinfectant for the skin. All parts of the plant are considered poisonous.

Mountain laurel prefers part shade and moist rocky or sandy soils. It is a lovely plant for the mid-Atlantic garden.

Mountain Laurel by Karen Ringstrand

Mountain Woodsorrel by Carol Woodin

Mountain Woodsorrel

Oxalis montana
Oxalidaceae (Woodsorrel Family)

Mountain woodsorrel is largely restricted to cool mountain forests in the mid-Atlantic region. It is often found in mountain seeps and mossy ledges. The five notched petals of the white or pink flowers have distinct pink veins. Flowers close as evening arrives. The leaves are clover-like and heart-shaped. The attractive foliage often persists after flowering. The fruit is a unique oblong, five-sided capsule and resembles a miniature tropical star fruit.

The woodsorrel family is small with only three genera and about nine hundred species. Most of the family is tropical, with a few temperate species including several sorrels. The widest range of mountain woodsorrel is between New England and the Great Lakes region. Distribution in the mid Atlantic is spotty through the highlands of the Allegheny and Great Smoky mountains. This suggests that woodsorrel is a truly northern species with relict populations along the relatively cool backbone of the Appalachians. Native Americans used the leaves as flavoring and a yellow dye. The flowers and leaves, though mildly toxic, may be eaten in small quantities or brewed into tea. Mountain woodsorrel is difficult to grow in the garden.

Muscadine

Vitis rotundifolia
Vitaceae (Grape Family)

Muscadine is a prolific grapevine found in many habitats of the southern half of the United States, as far west as Oklahoma and as far north as Delaware. Muscadine has curly tendrils allowing it to climb high into trees and on buildings. Its toothed leaves are 2 to 3 inches in length and its flowers are small and easily overlooked. The thick-skinned grapes are large with only a few grapes in a bunch. Most muscadine turns purple when it ripens in September and October; however, the scuppernong variety shown in the painting turns greenish-bronze in fall. The vines may reach lengths of 90 feet or more.

The grape family is composed mainly of woody vines. The economic importance of the family is ancient and globally significant as a source of food and wine. Native Americans ate the fruit of muscadine. It is a good source of food for birds and mammals. Early European settlers domesticated the muscadine, because European grape varieties did not thrive in the United States. The grape is used to make wine and preserves.

Muscadine is not often found in gardens, unless grown for its fruit. It can, under certain conditions, become aggressive.

Plants in the grape family serve as caterpillar hosts for the Abbott's Sphinx moth (*Sphecodina abbottii*), which has a wingspan of 2 to 2¾ inches. Painting by Kandy Phillips.

Muscadine by Kristie Bruzenak

Oakleaf Hydrangea

Hydrangea quercifolia
Hydrangeaceae (Hydrangea Family)

Oakleaf hydrangea is a native that provides year-round interest. Its panicles of white flowers, which appear in late June, develop a dark pinkish hue in autumn. The dark green lobed leaves, resembling large oak leaves, give a spectacular show in the fall when they turn red and purple. The exfoliating cinnamon-colored bark provides winter interest. Growing in height from 4 to 6 feet with equal or greater spread, this shrub is native to the southernmost portion of the mid Atlantic.

Hydrangeaceae include woody plants and vines that grow mainly in the northern hemisphere. Oakleaf hydrangea makes a lovely shrub for the garden and can be grown farther north than its native territory. Favoring partial shade to sun, this shrub likes average to moist soil and benefits from periodic watering during the dry summer months. The flowers are often used in dried arrangements.

The Mourning Cloak butterfly (*Nymphalis antiopa*) has a wingspan of 2¼ to 4 inches. Living as long as 10 to 11 months, it feeds on tree sap, rotting fruit, and some nectar. It might easily be found sunning itself after hibernation on a big leaf of *Hydrangea quercifolia*. Painting by Kandy Phillips.

Oakleaf Hydrangea by Barbara Jaynes

Pawpaw by Bonnie S. Driggers

Pawpaw

Asimina triloba
Annonaceae (Custard Apple Family)

The pawpaw stands alone in the mid-Atlantic flora for its fruits. No other native tree produces a larger, more delicious berry. The mild flavor of the fruit is similar to banana or melon, with a texture like custard. Appearing before the leaves, the fleshy, maroon flowers grow close to the branches. Although quite interesting, the flowers can be easily missed because of their dark color. A lover of moist sites, pawpaw is common along river edges in the mid Atlantic. In many locations along the Potomac and James rivers in Virginia, it is now prolific. Growing from spreading shoots, pawpaw can be the dominant lower canopy tree.

With 120 genera and 2,000 species, Annonaceae are a large family of mainly tropical trees and shrubs. The family is well represented in Amazonia and Central America, as well as Asia and Africa. The genus *Asimina* has several species; however, only two occur in the mid Atlantic. The family is the source of many fine fruits and perfumes. Pawpaw is a larval host for the Zebra Swallowtail butterfly (*Eurytides marcellus*) shown here and the Pawpaw Sphinx moth (*Dolba hyloeus*). Birds and small mammals enjoy the banana-like fruit. Native Americans ate the fruit both fresh and dried and used the inner bark of the pawpaw to make rope.

Pawpaw makes a good understory tree, growing from 10 to 40 feet tall. The trees require cross-pollination for good fruit production.

Zebra Swallowtail butterflies (*Eurytides marcellus*) use pawpaws as caterpillar hosts. Their wingspan is 2½ to 4 inches. Paintings by Kandy Phillips.

Pickerelweed by Vicki Malone

Pickerelweed

Pontederia cordata
Pontederiaceae
(Water Hyacinth Family)

Found growing in shallow water, pickerelweed stands out as both beautiful and ecologically important. The small blue to purple flowers are borne on compact spikes, and the attractive leaves are waxy and arrow-shaped. In large colonies pickerelweed is an excellent biological filter and slows sedimentation of shallow ponds. Pickerelweed is native to the eastern half of North America from Florida into Canada.

The small, strictly aquatic pickerelweed family is found in Asia, Africa, and the Americas. The closely related water hyacinth is invasive in the United States. The leaves of pickerelweed are a favorite haunt of dragonflies; the Blue Dasher (*Pachydiplax longipennis*) is shown in the painting. Many bee and butterfly species, such as the Silver-spotted Skipper butterfly (*Epargyreus clarus*) also shown in the painting, visit the flowers. One particular species of bee, the *Dufourea novaeangliae*, depends solely on pickerelweed pollen.

The seeds of the pickerelweed may be eaten raw, and the young leaf stalks, cooked. This 3-foot-tall aquatic plant tolerates small pond planting in home gardens but is highly attractive to deer. While native to the Americas, pickerelweed can be aggressive in some locations.

Pink Azalea

Rhododendron periclymenoides
Ericaceae (Heath Family)

The clusters of fragrant blossoms of the pink azalea appear in late spring before the leaves. The long, darker pink stamens emerge far beyond the pink petals, giving the blossoms a dramatic grace. Bright green leaves turn pale yellow and orange in autumn. This long-branched shrub will grow up to 6 feet. In the wild, pink azalea, which grows in a variety of conditions from sloped infertile soils to rich moist soils, can sometimes be found growing along stream banks.

The heath family has over 3,000 species widely distributed throughout the world. Small fruiting shrubs, such as cranberries and blueberries, are members of this family. The pink azalea has various common names including wild azalea and pinxterbloom. In Dutch, "Pinxter" loosely translates to Pentecost; the bloom time for the pinxterbloom was roughly the seventh Sunday after Easter.

Grown in the garden, this native can provide an alternative to the largely Asian cultivars that are normally seen. Because of its shallow root system, gardeners should keep the soil mulched and free from groundcover.

Pink Azalea by Mary Jane Zander

Possumhaw Viburnum

Viburnum nudum
Adoxaceae (Moschatel Family)

Clusters of creamy white flowers envelop this shrub in early summer, providing nectar and pollen for bumblebees and butterflies. The flower cluster is made up of tiny individual flowers with a pleasant fragrance. The foliage is more lustrous than that of other viburnums. In autumn, the leaves turn lovely shades of red and indigo. The small berries, botanically named "drupes," ripen by late summer, changing from ivory to pink to dark blue. Although two plants are not essential, cross-pollination and fruit production are better with more than one plant.

With fewer than 200 species, the moschatel family, also referred to as the elderberry family, includes shrubs and vines with an opposite leaf arrangement on the stem. Possumhaw viburnum provides wildlife with a good source of food and cover. Native Americans used the berries for food and the root bark as a tonic.

Growing along the Eastern Seaboard of North America, *Viburnum nudum* prefers partial to full sun and organically rich, acidic soil. It is often found growing near water sources. Normally reaching heights from 10 to 15 feet, cultivars such as 'Brandywine' and 'Winterthur' offer gardeners compact versions of this delightful viburnum.

The Red-spotted Purple butterfly (*Limenitis arthemis*) obtains nectar from the small white viburnum flowers. Adults have a wingspan of 2¼ to 4 inches. Painting by Kandy Phillips.

Possumhaw Viburnum by Mary Page Hickey

Purple Pitcher Plant by Pamela Mason

Purple Pitcher Plant

Sarracenia purpurea
Sarraceniaceae (Pitcher Plant Family)

The purple pitcher plant is one of the few carnivorous species in North America. A botanical curiosity, purple pitcher plant is unmistakable for its appearance. A single, large umbrella-like reddish flower nods over the rosette of unusual tubular leaves. The leaf opening has a strongly recurved lip with hairs pointing downward into the water-filled cavity. This design evolved to trap insects. In the wild, *Sarracenia purpurea* grows almost exclusively in *Sphagnum* bogs, highly specific habitats easily disturbed by human impact. Unsurprisingly, the distribution of the pitcher plant today is spotty in the mid Atlantic but very broad in the relatively undisturbed bog lands of central and eastern Canada.

The pitcher plant family is small, found only in the Americas, with most species occurring in the eastern United States. Native Americans found many medicinal uses for the plant, including treating gynecological disorders and urinary problems. They used the leaf as a drinking cup and children used the leaf as a toy kettle.

Most species can be readily cultivated given the right soil conditions and plenty of sun. Several are endangered or threatened.

Riverbank Grape by Berit Robertson

Riverbank Grape

Vitis riparia
Vitaceae (Grape Family)

Riverbank grape is closely related to the muscadine grape, but with a much wider continental distribution, particularly in the north of the United States and in Canada. It is usually found growing along streams, as indicated by its common and Latin names. While growth habits are similar, riverbank grape has a slightly larger leaf with three discrete lobes. The plant's vines easily reach lengths of 35 feet, but even 75 feet is possible. Like all native grapes, the yellow-green fragrant flowers are small and easily overlooked. The fruit is bluish black. The grapes are rarely seen, however, because the fruit is often high up on the climbing vine, and birds make quick work of eating them.

Native Americans ate the fruit of riverbank grape. They also soaked the vines in water, then used them to make baskets and to bind the poles used to construct wigwams and longhouses. Today, *Vitis riparia* is used as a rootstock for the wine grape, *Vinis vinifera*. When European vines were severely damaged by the aphid-like pest phylloxera, winemakers began grafting European grapes onto roots of native American grapes, such as *Vitis riparia*, which are resistant to phylloxera.

Riverbank grape is not often grown in gardens. Like muscadine, it can become aggressive.

The Pandorus Sphinx moth (*Eumorpha pandorus*), with a wingspan of 3¼ to 4½ inches, lays eggs on grape and Virginia creeper leaves, which provide food for the hatched caterpillars. Painting by Kandy Phillips.

Roundleaf Greenbrier

Smilax rotundifolia
Smilacaceae (Catbrier Family)

Throughout the mid Atlantic, roundleaf greenbrier is known to hikers and gardeners for two particular traits: its widespread distribution and sharp spines. Common along mountain trails in national forests and parks, greenbrier forms thickets and climbs into smaller trees. The dark green leathery leaves have deep-set parallel venation and a smooth margin. They are heart shaped and rarely more than 2 inches in length. Often overlooked, greenbrier flowers have a distinct vase-like shape. With the advent of fall, the plant produces small blue berries. In winter the delicate but persistent tendrils can be observed emerging from the green stem.

Native Americans used the greenbrier root for food and the leaves to treat skin ailments. The fruit, which persists into winter, is especially useful to wintering birds, such as the Northern Cardinal. The dense thickets of the roundleaf greenbrier, with their sharp spines, provide useful cover for small mammals and birds.

Roundleaf greenbrier is not suitable for the garden, because it is considered too aggressive.

The Curve-lined Owlet moth (*Phyprosopus callitrichoides*) has a wingspan of approximately $1^{1}/_{8}$ to $1^{3}/_{8}$ inches. Its remarkable caterpillar feeds on various greenbrier species. Paintings by Kandy Phillips.

Roundleaf Greenbrier by Rose Pellicano

Royal Fern by Corinne Lapin-Cohen

Royal Fern

Osmunda regalis
Osmundaceae (Royal Fern Family)

Found throughout the eastern United States, royal ferns are common in wet forests and seeps. The royal fern is a primitive and beautiful plant. The large fronds routinely grow to 3 feet. In early spring compact fiddleheads will emerge in large numbers. Royal fern produces a large cinnamon-gold-colored fertile frond in mid spring, shown on the right in the painting. The colorful fertile frond stands out from the handsome green foliage. Black crowns of rhizomes persist through winter.

The royal fern family is nearly global in distribution with many temperate and tropical species. In the wild, royal ferns play an important role in filtering water and stabilizing flooded soils. The fibrous root masses are sometimes collected and used as an orchid-growing medium. Native Americans of the Eastern Seaboard made a concoction of the fronds for treating kidney ailments.

In the garden, royal ferns are widely used as specimens or in mass plantings on wet soils. They may be grown in containers if provided with enough water. Like nearly all ferns, royal ferns are unpalatable to deer.

Showy Lady's Slipper

Cypripedium reginae
Orchidaceae (Orchid Family)

The regal showy lady's slipper is rare in the broadleaf forests of the mid Atlantic. Larger and more dramatic than the closely related moccasin flower, the showy lady's slipper has a pink flower and white sepals. The clasping leaves almost surround a stout, hairy stem. The foliage and stems can cause a considerable rash. In the mid Atlantic, distribution of showy lady's slipper is sporadic and populations are small. In Virginia, the plant is reported in only five counties, three in the northwest and two in the southwest. The mountains of North Carolina and Tennessee also host populations.

At home in limestone soils, swamps, and cool forests, showy lady's slipper is difficult to grow from *in vitro* propagated seedlings and, therefore, very rarely found in garden collections. Like most of the lady's slipper orchids, showy lady's slipper maintains a complex fungal relationship with soils and is easily disturbed. The plants should never be collected in the wild.

Showy Lady's Slipper by Carol Woodin

Showy Orchid by Judith M. Simon

Showy Orchid

Galearis spectabilis
Orchidaceae (Orchid Family)

With a wide distribution, from Maine to Missouri and Texas to Georgia, showy orchid is found only in more mature hardwood forests. Preferring rocky slopes with rich soil and dappled shade, it is unmistakable once spied on the forest floor. The basal leaves are broad and tongue-like with a uniform surface and smooth margin. From the center, a flowering stalk emerges in mid spring bearing two to fifteen flowers. The flower is enchanting, with purple helmet-like fused sepals arching over soft white lower petals. Slightly fragrant, it is popular with several bee species.

Part of the orchid family, the genus *Galearis* is named from the Latin word for helmet, which describes the shape of the upper hooded sepals. It is said that the showy orchid can be grown from seed. However, it is rarely available commercially and should be enjoyed in the wild. Like most orchids, its soil conditions are exacting and drainage is important. Growing from a fleshy root, it needs consistent moisture and copious leaf litter.

Skunk Cabbage by Kitty Gilbert

Skunk Cabbage

Symplocarpus foetidus
Araceae (Arum Family)

From the mid Atlantic north, no other plant announces the arrival of spring more emphatically than skunk cabbage. Rising from wet soils and swamp margins, its curious flower is often overlooked once the huge leaves appear. The initial flowering takes the form of a hood-like purple spathe enclosing the upright spadix. The spathe's warm darkness and carrion smell attract its insect pollinators. Although large, the flower often blends in with leaf litter. Once the leaves emerge, there is no mistaking this fascinating plant. The lime-green foliage stands out dramatically from an otherwise barren forest floor. The plant is a rare example of thermogenesis, creating its own warmth that can even melt surrounding snow. In much of its range, one can walk into damp forested ravines and be greeted by the seemingly tropical leaves, even as trees remain bare.

The arum family is a largely tropical group. The trademark reproductive organ of the arum family, the spadix is a club-like structure of tiny flowers, consistent throughout the family. Native Americans used the leaves and roots of the skunk cabbage to treat many ailments, including worms, coughs, and epilepsy.

Skunk cabbage is largely absent from public garden collections and most private gardens. The entire plant is malodorous, particularly when the foliage is crushed or bruised.

Smooth Solomon's Seal by Eileen Malone-Brown

Smooth Solomon's Seal

Polygonatum biflorum
Asparagaceae (Asparagus Family)

Found growing in rich, moist deciduous forests, smooth Solomon's seal usually appears in profusion and creates a lovely display. Attractive, deeply veined leaves clasp an arching stem that may extend several feet in length. By late April, pairs of pendulous, bell-shaped creamy flowers, tinged with green, dangle from the leaf axils. Dark blue pea-like berries that follow in late summer are enjoyed by birds and small mammals.

Smooth Solomon's seal is a woodland member of the diverse and populous asparagus family. One of several explanations for the derivation of the common name is that the flat circular stem scars on the root resemble the seal on the ring of the biblical King Solomon. Native Americans found many uses for the root: they used it and young shoots for food; they burned it for its fragrance; and they used it to treat stomach troubles and cuts.

Easy to grow in the garden, this perennial prefers partial shade with a few hours of dappled sun.

Southern Arrowwood by Carol Ashton-Hergenhan

Southern Arrowwood

Viburnum dentatum
Adoxaceae (Moschatel Family)

The clusters of small white flowers of southern arrowwood emerge in late spring, and the toothed leaves appear in pairs along the arching stems. In autumn southern arrowwood produces clusters of dark blue-black berries, and the foliage turns to yellow or wine red. The shrub can grow to 6 to 8 feet.

Adoxaceae are a small family with only four genera, including elders as well as viburnums, and 150 to 200 species. Southern arrowwood provides food for birds and small mammals. It serves as a larval host for the Spring Azure butterfly. Woodland Indians used the long, straight branches for arrow shafts, giving the plant its common name.

Southern arrowwood is a wetland indicator species that reaches its best development in damp soils. In the garden it will grow in slightly drier conditions as well. After flowering, the fruits are attractive in their own right.

The Hummingbird Clearwing moth (*Hemaris thysbe*) has a wingspan of 1$^{9}/_{16}$ to 2$^{3}/_{16}$ inches. The moth gathers nectar from many flowers, such as honeysuckle, beebalm, lilac, phlox, blueberry, thistle, and others. Its larvae feed on a variety of viburnums. Painting by Kandy Phillips.

Southern Magnolia

Magnolia grandiflora
Magnoliaceae (Magnolia Family)

A native of the southern mid Atlantic, southern magnolia produces perfumed, showy, waxy-white flowers in early summer. This large, broadleaf evergreen tree continues blooming sporadically through late summer. The dark green, glossy leaves with a velvety, rust-colored underside are dramatic. Bright red seeds in a large capsule follow the flowers. With its handsome gray bark, this large tree is among the most beautiful native trees.

Magnoliaceae are one of the primitive flowering families whose fossil remains date back to the Tertiary Period (65 million to 2.6 million years ago). The family comprises aromatic trees and shrubs, including our native tuliptree. The large, evergreen, waxy leaves of southern magnolia are used in floral arrangements along with the dried seed heads. Andrew Jackson brought this species from Tennessee in 1830 to plant at the White House. Native Americans used the bark for medicinal purposes, and the wood is used today to make furniture and cabinetwork.

Hardy as far north as Philadelphia, southern magnolia has many cultivars, including 'Little Gem,' a dwarf form reaching 14 feet in height.

Southern Magnolia
by Clarissa Bonde

Swamp Milkweed by Candace Aburdene

Swamp Milkweed

Asclepias incarnata
Apocynaceae (Dogbane Family)

Swamp milkweed produces dense floral umbels of reddish-pink flowers in midsummer, and their delightful fragrance attracts a multitude of pollinators. The large seedpods, measuring up to 5 inches long, begin forming immediately after flowering. When the seeds are ripe, the pod opens to reveal a nest of silky hairs with the small brown seeds attached. Even a slight breeze carries the seeds away. This strong, upright perennial, which tends to grow in clumps and bloom in mid to late summer, reaches approximately 3 feet in height and prefers partial shade to full sun.

Swamp milkweed is a larval host for the Monarch butterfly (*Danaus plexippus*), as well as the Queen butterfly (*Danaus gilippus*). By feeding on the leaves that contain a milky, white toxic sap, the caterpillar becomes unpalatable to predators – a wonderful evolutionary defense for the butterfly. Native Americans used the flowering heads for food, the fiber to make twine, and the roots to treat kidney disorders.

Valuable in the garden for its appearance and its attractiveness to butterflies and hummingbirds, swamp milkweed is usually found in wet soil conditions, as indicated by its common name.

Shown from the top are the female and male Monarch butterflies (*Danaus plexippus*) and their caterpillar, which feeds only on milkweed. Monarch wingspans are 3 3/8 to 4 7/8 inches. At bottom is the Snowberry Clearwing moth (*Hemaris diffinis*), which mimics a hummingbird with a humming sound. Its wingspan is 1 1/4 to 2 inches. Caterpillar hosts include members of the dogbane family. Paintings by Kandy Phillips.

Sweetgum by Carol Ashton-Hergenhan

Sweetgum

Liquidambar styraciflua
Altingiaceae (Sweetgum Family)

Widely cultivated, sweetgum is an ornamental tree with a large native range. Found along the Eastern Seaboard and southeast, it is also found in California and into Mesoamerica. The five-lobed, star-shaped leaves are unique among trees in eastern North America. The fall foliage of sweetgum is deep red or purple. The rounded fruit is a capsule made up of individual seedpods fused at the base.

Liquidambar styraciflua belongs to a small family of flowering plants that are wind pollinated. Native Americans used sweetgum to treat wounds, dysentery, and coughs. The Cherokee chewed the hardened resin, which, although fragrant like the leaves, actually has a bitter taste. The hard wood is used widely to make furniture, cabinets, plywood, and boxes. The sweetgum is useful as a nesting site for birds and as a food source for birds and small mammals, and the fruit capsules are used for decoration.

Widely planted as a street tree, mature sweetgums have a broad crown and provide shade as well as fall color.

Luna moths (*Actias luna*) feed on winged sumac, persimmon, sweetgum, hickory, and walnut among others; their wingspans can be up to 4 inches. Shown here are the moth and its caterpillar. Paintings by Kandy Phillips.

Toadshade

Trillium sessile
Melanthiaceae (Bunchflower Family)

Toadshade is common in rich forests of the mid Atlantic. The flower is stalkless, emerging in early spring directly from the three mottled leaves, technically considered bracts by some. Leaves, sepals, and petals appear in groups of three, giving the plant its scientific name. Blooming in March and April, toadshade grows to a height of about 12 inches. Unlike most trilliums, the narrow upright petals hide the floral parts. The petals' reddish-brown hues combine with variable shades of green on the mottled leaves to reveal the complex artistry of plant biodiversity.

Native Americans used the crushed foliage of toadshade to treat boils. They also used the roots, which have astringent and antiseptic properties, for treating wounds.

Toadshade can be discreet and bold all at once in the cultivated shade garden, and a grouping provides a memorable sight in spring woodlands. Although the plant is difficult to propagate from seeds, new plants sprout readily from underground rhizomes and the plant is also available from plant nurseries. Toadshade is an aesthetic and ecological jewel of the mid-Atlantic flora.

Toadshade by Bonnie S. Driggers

Tuliptree by Marsha Ogden

Tuliptree

Liriodendron tulipifera
Magnoliaceae (Magnolia Family)

A tall, stately tree with distinctively shaped leaves, the tuliptree is like no other tree in the eastern forest. The dramatic, cupped flower shown in the painting blooms high in the tree in early summer. It is a favorite among butterflies and hummingbirds, although bees are its most important pollinator. The leaves turn golden yellow in the fall. Cone-shaped clusters of seed persist through winter. This fast-growing tree has a very straight trunk and is one of the tallest in the forest, reaching heights from 80 to 125 feet.

The trees and shrubs of Magnoliaceae produce showy, fragrant, and bold flowers. Native Americans on the East Coast used the straight trunks of the tuliptree to make canoes and cradles. They also used a decoction of the bark as a sedative and as a treatment for pinworm. Tuliptree is a larval host for the Eastern Tiger Swallowtail butterfly (*Papilio glaucus*) and the Tuliptree Silkmoth (*Callosamia angulifera*). The wood of the tuliptree is used to make furniture.

The tuliptree is resistant to termites. It grows well in deep, rich soil where there is uniform rainfall.

Tuliptrees serve as caterpillar hosts for the Tuliptree Silkmoth (*Callosamia angulifera*), which has a wingspan of $3\frac{1}{8}$ to $4\frac{5}{16}$ inches. Shown here are the female (left) and male (right). Paintings by Kandy Phillips.

Turk's-cap Lily

Lilium superbum
Liliaceae (Lily Family)

Turk's-cap lily is the largest and most dramatic of native lilies. Its range extends along most of the Atlantic Seaboard and into the Midwest. The strongly reflexed petals of the flower are distinctive and thought to resemble a traditional Turkish hat. Colored deep orange with brown spots, the flower is as beautiful as it is functional. The floral parts extend well beyond the petals to attract pollinators. Turk's-cap lilies grow to 6 feet and sport many flowers on a single plant. The flowers, nearly pendulous, nod toward the ground.

Global in distribution, the lily family is now relatively small after recent reclassifications based on genetic data. Often grown commercially as ornamentals, some plants in this family are poisonous to family pets, particularly cats. Native Americans made a soup from the underground tubers of the Turk's-cap lily.

This is a superb plant for any garden. Widely available commercially and easy to grow, Turk's-cap is ideal in the home garden or in a garden collection. It grows best in full sun. Like all lilies, it requires protection from deer. Soil should be kept consistently moist.

Turk's-cap Lily by Jeannetta vanRaalte

Twinleaf by Lara Call Gastinger

Twinleaf

Jeffersonia diphylla
Berberidaceae (Barberry Family)

At the first signs of spring, twinleaf flowers appear on the shady forest floor. The pure white petals of the flower encircle a green and yellow center. The blossom of *Jeffersonia diphylla* is very delicate and in rain or wind will quickly lose its petals. The unusual leaf resembles a pair of angel wings. A pale venation gives the leaf texture. A seedpod, said to resemble a teapot, appears after the flower. Twinleaf grows from the mid Atlantic into the Midwest, but it is not abundant and in some places, is endangered.

Jeffersonia diphylla was named in honor of Thomas Jefferson by his friend and fellow botanist, Benjamin Smith Barton. Jefferson planted twinleaf in his gardens at Monticello. Twinleaf is a member of the barberry family, which includes such non-native shrubs as nandina and Japanese barberry, both considered invasive pests in the mid Atlantic. The genus *Jeffersonia* has only one other species, *Jeffersonia dubia*, found in Japan. Native Americans found many uses for twinleaf, such as a poultice for sore muscles and a tea to treat liver ailments.

Twinleaf prefers a semi-shady area in rich forest soil and grows to about 12 inches in height. Although the flower lasts only a few days, twinleaf provides an attractive deciduous groundcover in a shaded area of the garden.

Virginia Rose

Rosa virginiana
Rosaceae (Rose Family)

Sometimes reaching 6 feet tall, Virginia rose is a stunning sight when in flower. Although the flowers are not long-lived, they are large and showy. The rose corolla is a pleasing shade of medium pink and about 2 inches across. The stems are hairy and thorns curiously curved. The fleshy hip can be orange or red. In the mid Atlantic, a close Asian relative, *Rosa multiflora*, is among the most pernicious invasive shrubs.

The rose family is large, with 120 genera and more than 3,300 species, including trees, shrubs, and perennials found worldwide. The family includes numerous important temperate food crops such as strawberries, raspberries, almonds, cherries, plums, apples, and peaches. The wood of many rose species is used for inlay and fine musical instruments. In addition, rose hips have a long ethno-botanic history. The hips are rich in vitamin C and can be used for jelly and tea. Native bees are attracted to the flowers of Virginia rose and the hips provide food for birds. Native Americans used a decoction of the roots for medicinal baths, and the buds for food.

The Stinging Rose Moth (*Parasa indetermina*) has a wingspan of $^{15}/_{16}$ to $1^{3}/_{16}$ inches. Its larvae feed on apples, dogwoods, hickories, maples, oaks, poplars, and rose bushes. The caterpillars have bristles that irritate and sting, hence the name. Paintings by Kandy Phillips.

Virginia Rose by Margaret Farr

Virginia Saltmarsh Mallow by Berit Robertson

Virginia Saltmarsh Mallow

Kosteletzkya virginica
Malvaceae (Mallow Family)

An exceptional bloomer in late summer, Virginia saltmarsh mallow is found along the coastal plains from New York to Texas. The pink flowers have five large petals and long yellow stamens. Virginia saltmarsh mallow forms attractive colonies. Tolerant of some salt, this perennial grows in damp areas and swamps but is absent from beach faces, the seaward slopes exposed to wave action.

Kosteletzkya is closely related to *Hibiscus* and shares a very similar floral anatomy. The mallow family is widespread. Cotton, okra, China jute, and many ornamental shrubs make the family economically important. Butterflies enjoy the large blossoms of Virginia saltmarsh mallow.

This shrub is an easy native for gardeners to grow in full sun. Once established, plants can tolerate drier conditions but should be well watered through the summer months.

Virginia Spiderwort by Karen Ringstrand

Virginia Spiderwort

Tradescantia virginiana
Commelinaceae (Spiderwort Family)

A superb native plant for the garden, Virginia spiderwort has beautiful flowers and fine upright foliage. The purple-blue flowers bloom early in the day and by nightfall they become jelly-like. The next day a new crop of flowers blooms. In the wild, they often prefer wet slopes and shady seeps. The common name derives from the arrangement of the leaves that is said to resemble a spider as seen from above. Linnaeus named this plant for John Tradescant the Elder, a celebrated English horticulturist of the seventeenth century.

The spiderwort family is mainly tropical in distribution with several species reaching the subtropics and mild temperate climes in the Americas. The family includes 13 genera and 1,200 species. Native Americans ate the young growth of the plant and used an infusion to treat stomachache and cancer. The flowers attract bees.

Spiderworts are commonly available, and there are a number of hybrid cultivars. Nearly all commercially named forms are crosses between *Tradescantia virginiana* and *T. ohiensis*. In sunnier conditions spiderwort will reach 3 feet in height.

White Fringetree

Chionanthus virginicus
Oleaceae (Olive Family)

White fringetree is one of the finest small trees in our native flora. In full bloom by mid May, the delicate flowers cover the tree in an aromatic white aura. The flower clusters contain a multitude of flowers with four to six ribbon-like petals. Dark green glossy leaves and gray bark banded in white create summer interest. By late summer the small dark blue fruits are abundant on female trees. Although male trees bear no fruit, they are often showier in bloom. Native birds are attracted to the fruit, which looks like a miniature olive.

The olive family is of economic and cultural importance due to the culinary olive, *Olea europaea*. Oleaceae also include jasmine, lilac, privet, forsythia, and ash. Cosmopolitan in distribution, the family has 29 genera and some 600 species. Native Americans used the bark of the white fringetree to treat wounds and bruises. Birds eat the berries, and the tree serves as a larval host for the Rustic Sphinx moth (*Manduca rustica*).

For the gardener, white fringetree has showy flowers, attractive foliage, and value to wildlife. Tolerant of variable soils, *Chionanthus virginicus* is easy to grow.

White Fringetree by Juliet Kirby

Winged Sumac by Rose Pellicano

Winged Sumac

Rhus copallinum
Anacardiaceae (Sumac Family)

Winged sumac is a tropical-looking shrub with compound leaves up to 1 foot in length and lance-shaped leaflets. Tops of leaves are shiny and dark green while the underside is fuzzy and paler. Panicles of green flowers in summer give way to clusters of red fruits that persist through winter. The foliage turns vivid red in the autumn. This native shrub can be found in fields and along roadsides and can grow up to 20 feet in height.

Anacardiaceae include such important plants as cashews, mangos, pistachios, and poison ivy. Native Americans used winged sumac to treat sunburns and other skin irritations. The edible berries from female plants were used to make dyes. In colonial times the European settlers used the berries of this species and other native sumacs to make a lemony-tasting drink called "Indian Lemonade." In addition, they used parts of the shrub for dyeing and for tanning animal skins. Small mammals and birds eat the fruit. Winged sumac is a host plant for the Spring Azure (*Celastrina ladon*) and Red-banded Hairstreak (*Calycopis cecrops*) butterflies.

Winged sumac, which tolerates full sun to partial shade, is very easy to grow. It grows in both acidic and alkaline soils and does well in drought conditions. This plant suckers, which makes it useful to grow on slopes for erosion control.

The Red-banded Hairstreak butterfly (*Calycopis cecrops*) lays its eggs on fallen sumac leaves. Its wingspan is only ⅞ to 1¼ inches. Painting by Kandy Phillips.

Yaupon and Possumhaw by Lotus McElfish

Yaupon and Possumhaw

Ilex vomitoria and *Ilex decidua*
Aquifoliaceae (Holly Family)

Yaupon is an evergreen holly with glossy, rounded leathery green leaves and red berries. Possumhaw, a deciduous holly, loses its leaves in the fall. Possumhaw berries vary in color from rich red to, more rarely, yellow and are quite conspicuous in winter on the bare branches. Yaupon distribution follows the Eastern Seaboard from Virginia to Texas. The possumhaw is found in the same area with a wider path inland from the coast and as far west as Kansas.

At least 400 species of trees and shrubs make up the holly family, with representatives on every continent except Antarctica. Native Americans brewed yaupon leaves to make a tea for ceremonial purposes. Other herbs were sometimes added to render the tea an emetic. Colonists believed it was the yaupon that gave the "black drink" its emetic qualities, which accounts for the Latin name. Native Americans also used yaupon to make arrows and ramrods. Yaupon and possumhaw are valuable to wildlife, offering nectar-rich flowers in spring and nutritious berries in the fall. Yaupon is a larval host for the Henry's Elfin butterfly (*Callophrys henrici*).

Hollies are very adaptable and these two are no exception. They prefer slightly acidic soils with full to partial sun. Popular as landscape plants, both hollies have been bred to produce variants including dwarf, weeping, and single-stem tree forms. The berries, botanically called drupes, have also been selected and cultivated to produce a range of colors from red to orange to yellow. The yaupon can be pruned into an attractive evergreen hedge.

Possumhaw serves as a caterpillar host for the Pawpaw Sphinx moth (*Dolba hyloeus*). The wingspan is 2 to $2^{11}/_{16}$ inches. Painting by Kandy Phillips.

Donors

· BENEFACTORS ·

Count & Countess Peder Bonde
Beck & Kitty Gilbert
Barbara Jaynes

· PATRONS ·

American Society of Botanical Artists
Esther Carpi
The Garden Club of Fairfax
Berit Robertson

· SUPPORTERS ·

Francesca Anderson
Susan Payson Burke
The Community Foundation for Northern Virginia – Alan M. & Nathalie P. Voorhees Fund
Gerald & Bonnie Driggers
Margaret Farr
Mary Page Hickey
Anne Lewis
Marcia Long
Karen Ringstrand
Robert & Judy Rodgers
Mary Lou Steptoe

· FRIENDS ·

Candace Aburdene
Sheri Appleby
Carol Ashton-Hergenhan
Marion Ballard
Botanical Art Society of the National Capital Region
Sara Joline Bedford
James C. & Elizabeth W. Carroll
Karen Coleman
Philip & Sara Davis
Essex County Adirondack Garden Club
Anne Feldman
Marjorie K. Greenawald
John L. King
Juliet Kirby
Page Hickey Klumpar & Family
Jerry Kurtzweg
Corinne Lapin-Cohen
Michael & Donna Lauer
Holly Maillet
Vicki Malone

Eileen Malone-Brown
Cynthia McCormick
Noël Miller
Barbara & Kendyl Monroe
Jean Morra
Barbara O. Mosby
Ruth Nussbaum
Carolyn K. Offutt
Marsha Ogden
Constance Paine
Steve Robertson
Christine H. Rollins
Karen Royce
Jessica Tcherepnine
Jeannetta vanRaalte
James Waggener
Elsa B. Williams
Alicia Fox Wynn
Patricia & Alfred Yergey
Mary Jane Zander

Artists

The artists represented in the book offer a few insights into their art. Visit their websites or inquire at baee.info@gmail.com to learn more about them.

Born and raised in Indiana along the shores of Lake Michigan, **CANDACE ABURDENE** has had a lifelong love of plants, nature, and gardening. Her beloved grandfather, an avid forager of edible plants, nurtured this love, while her mother encouraged her artistic talent. Candace developed a love of botanical art while living in London and when working as an interior designer. She now hopes to devote most of her time to botanical painting and to introduce her one-year-old grandson to the beautiful gardens and nature preserves in the Washington, D.C., area, where she currently resides with her husband, Odeh.

A graduate of the University of Michigan with a BS in Design, **INGRID ARNESEN** has pursued a career in graphic design. She has designed books, logos, programs, brochures, and stationery, as well as museum exhibits and theatrical sets. Ingrid's passion for gardening and garden design led to her interest in floral arrangement, then to her participation in international floral design competitions, and eventually to the study of botanical illustration. Ingrid has studied under master teachers Louisa Rawle Tiné, Joan Frain, and Anne-Marie Evans. Ingrid's illustration of *Cornus florida* was inspired by her love of the beautiful dogwood tree and her interest in keeping this threatened native plant in existence in the Northeast.

CAROL ASHTON-HERGENHAN received her bachelor's degree from the Philadelphia College of Art (now University of the Arts) and went on to study at Temple University's Tyler School of Art, eventually earning a masters' degree in media. She began showing her drawings and paintings after graduation but took a hiatus from exhibiting while she managed the in-house creative and media departments of several large corporations. She returned to fine art full time upon retirement in 2010. Carol is a Master Gardener, and plants have always been central to her art. In the past three years she has been in numerous juried and invitational botanical illustration exhibits as well as several national and international juried shows incorporating a wide range of styles and subjects.

CHIARA BECCHI lives and works in Brookside, New Jersey. A graduate of the New York Botanical Garden's Certificate Program in illustration, she works in watercolor, pen and ink, and color and graphite pencil. Born in Torino, Italy, in 1947, she has lived extensively abroad, in Africa and Europe. After obtaining a BA in studio art in the United States and a certificate in industrial design in Milan, Italy, she devoted herself to depicting and interpreting botanical subjects, in particular, native plants. Chiara is a member of ASBA, BASNCR, and a Fellow of the Brooklyn Botanic Garden's Florilegium Society.

SARA JOLINE BEDFORD divides her time between Cape Cod, Massachusetts, and London, England, where she earned a diploma in botanical illustration from the English Gardening School. She has exhibited paintings at Hampton Court Palace, Kew Gardens, the Hunt Institute in Pittsburgh, Pennsylvania, the Ebury Galleries in London, and the RHS Horticultural Halls, Westminster. Sara is a member of ASBA as well as a fellow member of the Hampton Court Palace Florilegium Society. She has contributed numerous paintings to the archive there. sara.bedford@btinternet.com

CLARISSA BONDE's work is in public and private collections in Europe and the United States. Her art has been shown in group exhibitions, and some paintings are on long-term exhibit at the USBG in Washington, D.C. Clarissa's botanical paintings have been displayed in solo exhibitions at the Corcoran College of Art + Design, the American Horticultural Society, the George Washington University Galleries, and the American Swedish Historical Museum. She worked as adjunct faculty of the Corcoran College of Art + Design and her art is included in the books, *Things as They Are*, by Leslie Exton, and the *Botanical Treasures of Lewis and Clark*, compiled by Leslie Exton, Jan Denton, and Wendy Cortesi. Clarissa served on the ASBA Board and currently is on the BAEE board of directors.

Originally hailing from the mid-Atlantic region, **KRISTIE BRUZENAK** is now a professor of Foundation Studies at the Savannah College of Art and Design in Savannah, Georgia. She studied classical drawing and design at the Barnstone Studios in Coplay, Pennsylvania, for seven years before earning her MFA degree at the Pennsylvania Academy of the Fine Arts in Philadelphia. It was at the Academy that she began incorporating plants in her compositions as spiritual symbols. Due to her recently developed interest in the tradition of botanical painting, she is studying with the Society of Botanical Artists in England. The scuppernong grape, a variety of *Vitis rotundifolia*, is an appropriate choice for her illustration because of its origin on the mid-Atlantic coast and its current presence in the coastal South. kebpainter@gmail.com

ESTHER CARPI worked as a design professional for many years before becoming a full-time artist in 2005. She is an active member of the Garden Club of Virginia, serving on the Horticulture Committee and as a regular contributor to their website. Her botanical illustrations have been exhibited at the USBG in Washington, D.C., the Athenaeum in Alexandria, and the Jefferson Library at Monticello. Esther earned a Certificate in Botanical Art from the Corcoran College of Art + Design. She studied botanical art and illustration with the renowned botanical art teachers Anne-Marie Evans, Jenny Phillips, and Wendy Hollender. She is a member of ASBA and BASNCR and currently serves on the board of directors for BAEE.

As an artist, **KAREN COLEMAN** is passionate about the world of plants and traditional botanical art. In 2010, Karen earned a Certificate from the Brookside Gardens School of Botanical Art and Illustration in Maryland, where she now teaches. Her work has been shown in many local and international exhibitions and is included in the permanent collection of the Hunt Institute for Botanical Documentation. She is a member of ASBA and BASNCR, and a Signature Member of the Colored Pencil Society of America. In her work, she strives to convey a sense of wonder and respect for the natural world, as well as a desire to protect what we have left.

A native Japanese artist, **TOMOKO HAMADA CONNOLLY** is professor of anthropology at the College of William and Mary. She studied sumi-e brush painting, calligraphy, and kimono-textile flower painting in Japan. In 1989, she moved to Williamsburg, where she met the botanical art teacher Juliet Kirby, under whose tutelage she has been painting since 1992. Tomoko has studied botanical illustration at the Kew Royal Botanic Gardens and West Dean College in England, and at the Lewis Ginter Botanical Gardens in Richmond, Virginia. Adopting the Buddhist approach to nature, she tries to capture the ephemeral nature of plant life with artistic grace, while appreciating the rigorous scientific tradition of illustrating nature accurately.

LEE BOULAY D'ZMURA is an award-winning botanical artist whose experience in landscape architecture enriches her art. The transition from landscape documentation, preservation, and design to botanical painting is a natural extension of her knowledge and love of plants. The fine detail in her paintings is in part the result of years of technical drawing. Lee received a Certificate from the Brookside Gardens School of Botanical Art and Illustration where she teaches advanced watercolor classes. A member of ASBA and BASNCR, she maintains a studio in St. Michaels where she draws inspiration from her neighbors' gardens and from the native wildflowers of Maryland's Eastern Shore. www.leedzmura.com

BONNIE S. DRIGGERS' love of plants began at a young age when her mother and grandmother imparted their knowledge of plants on walks in the woods; they seemed to know the names of every plant and its uses. In 2007, Bonnie arranged the first of many art classes taught by Anne-Marie Evans in Virginia. In 2011, she organized local artists into the nonprofit corporation BAEE and has served since then as President. Her work experience as a technical editor and publications manager helped prepare her for the BAEE book project. Her art has appeared in juried competitions in the United States and Scotland.

MARGARET ('BETSY') FARR was born in Macon, Georgia, attended Wesleyan College in Macon, and graduated from the University of North Carolina, Chapel Hill. She resides in Manassas, Virginia. Betsy's work is held by the Basilica of the National Shrine of Mary, Queen of the Universe, Orlando, Florida; Shirley Sherwood Collection of Contemporary Botanical Art, London; Hunt Institute for Botanical Documentation, Carnegie Mellon University; Denver Botanic Gardens; Brooklyn Botanic Garden; and St. Elizabeth Ann Seton Catholic Church, Lake Ridge, Virginia. Her work appears in *Today's Botanical Artists* (Shiffer Press, 2008) and *Contemporary Botanical Artists: The Shirley Sherwood Collection*. Betsy is represented by Gleedsville Art Publishers, Leesburg, Virginia. stellaclara@comcast.net

LARA CALL GASTINGER is the chief illustrator for the recently published *Flora of Virginia*, a botanical reference manual that contains 1,300 of her original illustrations. She earned an undergraduate degree in Biology from the University of Virginia and a master's degree in plant ecology from Virginia Polytechnic Institute and State University. She is a member of ASBA, McGuffey Art Center, and the Virginia Native Plant Society. She has exhibited in New York City and at the Royal Horticultural Society show in

London where she was awarded with the highest honor of a gold medal. Her work has been accepted into the prestigious Hunt Institute for Botanical Documentation. She is represented by Susan Frei Nathan Fine Works on Paper. www.laracallgastinger.com

After a career as an editor at the Metropolitan Museum, **KITTY GILBERT** took up botanical painting. A member of ASBA, BAEE, and NESBA, she has studied at the New York Botanical Garden and with the brilliant teacher Anne-Marie Evans.

Having painted botanical watercolors for the last 18 years, **MARY PAGE HICKEY** continues studying under Anne-Marie Evans. Mary Page has also worked as a horticultural consultant for both public and private clients. Her love of nature and plants was greatly influenced by her family and has focused her quest for perfection in illustrating artistically not only the botanical aspects of various plants but also their unique traits. She has exhibited at the Garden Club of America headquarters in New York; the Athenaeum in Alexandria, Virginia; and often at the High Peaks Art Show in Keene Valley, New York. She is a member of ASBA, BASNCR, and the board of directors of BAEE. The Garden Club of America awarded her the prestigious Horticultural Arts Award in 2012.

BARBARA JAYNE's love of the beauty and intricacy of flowers, and her sadness at how quickly they die, leads her to preserve them on paper. Anne-Marie Evans, with whom she studies botanical watercolor, asked if she would like to submit a painting for the BAEE project. Rather ambitiously, she selected the *Hydrangea quercifolia*. Barbara's art has been exhibited at the Lincoln Cathedral, in England, and a painting was chosen for the Virginia Robinson Gardens Florilegium in California.

JULIET KIRBY grew up in England and studied fine art in London. She emigrated to the United States in 1958 and, after creating four children, returned to art in 1989 at the New York Botanical Garden. She graduated with a Certificate in Botanical Art. In 1996, Juliet moved to Williamsburg, Virginia, and started teaching botanical art at This Century Art Gallery in Williamsburg and at Lewis Ginter Botanical Gardens in Richmond. Juliet participates in many group art and botanical art shows both in Virginia and in Washington, D.C. Her work is in many private collections in the United States and England. She is a member of ASBA, BASNCR, and BAEE.

JERRY KURTZWEG has spent his career working on environmental issues. Botanical art provides Jerry with the opportunity to combine his interest in the environment with two other interests, North American history and art. In his artwork, Jerry focuses on native plants, particularly those of the mid-Atlantic region and the Pacific Northwest. Jerry studied botanical art at the Corcoran College of Art + Design and the Brookside Gardens School of Botanical Art and Illustration. His artwork has been included in a number of juried exhibitions.

"I try to reveal what is hidden – to help you see what you've never noticed before – the beauty in truth." An art major in college, **CORINNE LAPIN-COHEN** studied botanical art with Anne-Marie Evans in England, and earned a Certificate in Botanical Art from the NYBG. For the last 15 years, she has been teaching the art of botanical drawing and painting at the New York Botanical Garden, Lehman College, Lasdon Arboretum, and Stonehouse Studio. Corinne's watercolor paintings and metalpoint drawings are exhibited in museums, hospitals, arboretums, and galleries throughout the country. Her work is in the permanent collection of the Hunt Institute for Botanical Documentation, and has been published in numerous magazines and books. www.corinnelapincohen.com

Born in Chicago, **MARCIA LONG** decided to be an artist when her kindergarten drawing of Three Snowmen was published in the school newspaper. She received a scholarship to the Art Institute of Chicago, and majored in art at The Ohio State University, where she earned certification to teach art. Marcia studied botanical art with Anne-Marie Evans in Master Classes at the New York Botanical Garden; at Filoli in Woodside, California; in Falls Church, Virginia; and in New York City; as well as with other teachers at St. Michaels, Maryland; Brookside Botanical Gardens, Maryland; Phipps Conservatory and Botanical Gardens, Pittsburgh; and the Ringling College of Art and Design, Sarasota, Florida. Currently, Mrs. Long is an artist with the Colonial Williamsburg Foundation. She resides with her husband, Lawrence, and Himalayan cat, Mr. Tipperton, in Williamsburg, Virginia.

HOLLY HOVEN MAILLET received her BA in human biology at Stanford University in 1983. For ten years, she and her family lived in Japan, Hong Kong, and Singapore where she taught art classes and ran a successful business painting murals and commissioned pieces. Upon returning to the United States in 1998, Holly combined her artistic talent with her evolving interest in the natural world and the healing power of plants, studying at the Brooklyn

Botanic Garden and completing the Certificate program in botanical art and illustration at the New York Botanical Garden. Today, she lives in Charlottesville, Virginia, where she focuses on commissioned botanical painting, writing, and creating a recently launched line of note cards. Holly is a member of ASBA, BASNCR, and Central Virginia Botanical Artists. ehmaillet@gmail.com

EILEEN MALONE-BROWN received her Certificate in Botanical Art and Illustration from the Corcoran College of Art + Design in 2010. Eileen's garden serves as the primary source of her inspiration, since she prefers to draw and paint what she grows and can easily observe. Over the past decade, Eileen incorporated more mid-Atlantic native plants into her garden with very satisfying results. She also enjoys researching each plant's history and its uses, particularly those plants with medicinal qualities. Eileen is a member of ASBA and BASNCR. Her work has been shown at Monticello's Jefferson Library, the Delaware Art Museum, and Alexandria's Athenaeum.

VICKI MALONE earned a BFA from the University of Kansas. She worked for many years in the graphic arts, public relations, and the culinary arts (most recently as a personal chef and caterer). She received a Certificate in Botanical Art and Illustration from the Corcoran School of Art + Design and the USBG in Washington, D.C. While studying at the Corcoran, Vicki won the Kenneth Stubbs Memorial Award for excellence in drawing and painting. She is a member of ASBA and BASNCR. Her work has been shown at the Corcoran Museum, USBG, Monticello Library, and galleries in the mid-Atlantic region.

PAMELA R. MASON began studying art in 2006 at the Brookside Gardens School of Botanical Art and Illustration in Maryland, under director Margaret Saul. She completed the two-year program of coursework and has taken workshops with artists such as Anne-Marie Evans, Billy Showell, Mindy Lighthipe, John Pastoriza-Piñol, Kandy Phillips, and Martha Kemp. A past President of BASNCR, Pamela is also a member of ASBA. She has exhibited in juried group shows at the Athenaeum and River Farm, both in Alexandria, Virginia, and at Brookside Gardens. Her artwork has appeared in *The Botanical Artist*, the journal of ASBA.

A lifelong, self-taught artist and certified aromatherapist, **LOTUS MCELFISH** focused on her enchantment with botanicals in 2004. Born in Colorado, she resides in the Texas hill country, observing as development encroaches on the natural habitat of native plants. A 2005 ASBA grant led her on a marvelous journey of documenting Rare and Endangered Plants, and today she engages people with her art for conservation purposes. She shares her journey of finding and creating these plant portraits with a public talk and slide show. According to Lotus, "It's about discovery. Even the simplest plant unveils a complexity that . . . astonishes me. I want scientific accuracy, but I also want the viewer to see the magic of its existence."
www.lotusmcelfish.com

Entering the world of botanical art after a long career in publications and communications in the Washington, D.C., area, **MARSHA OGDEN** studied at the Brookside Gardens School of Botanical Art and Illustration in Maryland and with internationally known botanical artists. Her portrayal of the intriguing, fragile, and fleeting nature of living things directly from live material mirrors the truth and beauty of each subject. She focuses on mid-Atlantic specimens, the flora of New England, and tropical beauties of Hawaii. In juried exhibitions of BASNCR in 2010 and 2012, Marsha won the People's Choice Award for "Miniature Roses" and "Bleeding Hearts." Her artwork is held in several private collections. She is an active member of ASBA; a board member of BASNCR, having edited its newsletter from 2008-2010; and BAEE.
www.botanicalartstudio.com

ANNIE PATTERSON began botanical painting after a long career as a graphic designer. This new direction enabled her to combine painting and her fascination with collecting and growing plants. Now she lives in France where, because growing conditions are different, she enjoys the challenge of painting new subjects. When Annie looked at the native mid-Atlantic plant lists, she thought it would be easy to choose subjects. Then came the task of actually finding specimens in France, and she realized her choices were going to be rather limited due to growing conditions and availability. She narrowed her choices down to *Lobelia cardinalis* with its interestingly constructed, intense red flowers and the understated *Saururus cernuus*, the lizard's tail.
www.botanicalannie.co.uk

ROSE PELLICANO began to focus on botanical painting in 1993, and since then her work has appeared in ASBA exhibitions at The Horticultural Society of New York; the USBG, Washington D.C.; the New York Botanical Garden; and the Weisman Art Museum in Minneapolis. Other exhibitions include the Bruce Museum; Filoli; The Hunt Institute for Botanical Documentation; The Royal Horticultural Society, London; and more recently the Losing Paradise? exhibition at various national venues, including the Smithsonian Institution in Washington, D.C. Rose is a member of the Brooklyn Botanic Garden Florilegium Society. Her work has been published in magazines and in the book *Today's Botanical Artists*. She served on the Board of ASBA and currently teaches botanical painting. She is represented by Susan Frei Nathan Fine Works on Paper and Sunflower Gallery. pellicanor@optonline.net

KANDY VERMEER PHILLIPS studied at the Chicago Academy of Fine Arts. She has a lifelong interest in nature and medieval illumination. She received an ASBA Artist's Grant for her project researching the materials and techniques of manuscript painting. Kandy recently received the Don and Virginia Eckelberry Fellowship to study birds in medieval manuscripts. Kandy volunteers in the Department of Entomology at the Smithsonian National Museum of Natural History where she curates moths. She has also illustrated for scientific publications in entomology and invertebrate zoology. Kandy has received awards in numerous juried shows. Her works are included in private and public collections, including The Hunt Institute for Botanical Documentation, where a number of her illuminations were included in their 13th International Exhibition of Botanical Art & Illustration in 2010 and in their What We Collect exhibition in 2013.

A landscape architect, student of art history and botany, **CYNTHIA RICE** recently added the title "botanical artist." Having grown up in the woods and fields of Vermont and the Adirondack mountains, she has always had a special interest in mid-Atlantic native plants. As a gardener, she has learned they are the ones that thrive in their native habitat and blend effortlessly in the landscape. Sharing the endless discoveries that flow from close observation of these plants is, for her, one of the great rewards of botanical art.

Having no previous training in art, **KAREN RINGSTRAND** began painting when she enrolled in an adult education course titled Oil Painting for Beginners in the 1990s, in London. An article in the *Financial Times* prompted her to enroll in a botanical art class taught by Anne-Marie Evans at the Chelsea Physic Garden. After receiving her diploma there, Karen helped organize and took part in a group exhibition of botanical watercolors at the Mall Galleries, London, in September 2005. Moving to the Washington, D.C., area in 2008, Karen has continued to paint and take classes. She has focused her painting for this project on plants found in woodlands near her home in northern Virginia. Karen has taken an active role in BAEE, as Board member and Treasurer. kringstrand@aya.yale.edu

It was easy for **BERIT ROBERTSON** to choose the plants she painted for this project: the Virginia saltmarsh mallow grows outside the window of her house on the Eastern Shore of Maryland, and the riverbank grape flourishes along the banks of the Potomac River, where she takes walks. Berit came late to botanical art, earning her Certificate at the Brookside Gardens School of Botanical Art and Illustration in Maryland after an earlier degree in interior design. She has exhibited in juried shows at Brookside Gardens and at several Virginia locations: River Farm; the Athenaeum; the National Arboretum, where she received the People's Choice Award; and at Green Spring Gardens. Berit is a member of ASBA, BASNCR, and The Garden Club of America.

Relatively new to botanical art, **JUDY RODGERS** is particularly interested in native plants as art subjects as well as in their protection and preservation. Learning about the BAEE project through classes with Anne-Marie Evans, Judy strongly supports the project's goals to increase awareness and conservation as well as to further botanical art education and support botanical gardens. Judy is a member of ASBA, BASNCR, and the Central Virginia Botanical Artists. She is on the BAEE board of directors. She has studied at the Brookside Gardens School of Botanical Art and Illustration in Maryland and is enrolled in the Lewis Ginter Botanical Garden Certificate program in Richmond.

JUDITH SIMON practices botanical art in Berks County, Pennsylvania. She has a BFA in communication design with a concentration in illustration from Kutztown University. An avid organic gardener and plant collector, she combines gardening with botanical art and illustration. Judy also enjoys seeking out native plants in their environment, especially those with interesting forms and textures. A member of ASBA and PSBI, she currently chairs the PSBI exhibition committee at the 2014 Philadelphia Flower show. Exhibitions include the Philadelphia Flower Show, the 13th and 15th annual HSNY/ASBA show, Following in the Bartrams' Footsteps, Jenkins Arboretum, Friends Hospital, and Winterthur Museum.

ALICE TANGERINI has been the Staff Illustrator for the Botany Department, National Museum of Natural History at the Smithsonian Institution, since 1972. She has illustrated over 1,500 species of plants, mostly in pen and brush with ink and graphite and digital color. Her illustrations have appeared in scientific periodicals, floras, and books. Typically, she uses dried herbarium specimens, but assignments have taken her to California, Hawaii, and Guyana where she was able to draw from living material. She has taught classes and exhibited her artwork at botanical gardens, universities, and other museums. Alice also manages and curates a collection of botanical illustrations in her department. See a portion of this collection at http://botany.si.edu/botart. TANGERIN@si.edu

A self-taught botanical artist **JESSICA TCHEREPNINE** has painted flowers all her life, loving the detailed observation this requires. She has had solo exhibitions in London, New York, Paris, and Palm Beach, and has been included in numerous group exhibitions. The RHS has awarded her two Gold Medals. Jessica is a founding member of ASBA, and has been invited to paint for the Highgrove Florilegium, and the Filoli and the Brooklyn Botanic Garden florilegia. Some international collections that include her work are those of the Hunt Institute for Botanical Documentation, The British Museum (Natural History), the Royal Horticultural Society, Lindley Library, and the Dr. Shirley Sherwood Collection.

JUDITH TOWERS' career as a middle school art teacher provided little time to pursue her interest in plants, particularly those which provide fiber and color for handspinners, handweavers, and natural dyers. She has a BA in art education from Madison College, now James Madison University. After retiring in 2000, Judith earned a Botanical Illustration Certificate from LGBG in Richmond, Virginia. Her work has been exhibited at gardens, art centers, and libraries in the Richmond area and in Williamsburg. She prefers to work with watercolor and graphite pencil. She is an ASBA member and one of the founding members of Central Virginia Botanical Artists, an ASBA Circle.

JEANNETTA VAN RAALTE, a native New Yorker, studied fine art and graphic design at Cooper Union and New York University, and textile design at Parsons. For many years, she worked as a textile designer in home furnishings. After seeing an exhibition of botanical paintings, she began painting botanical subjects. Her paintings have been in many juried exhibitions and some are in the permanent collections of the Hunt Institute for Botanical Documentation and the New York State Museum. She considers the BAEE project to be wonderful and is grateful that she found a beautiful specimen of a Turk's-cap lily to contribute. She spends most of her time painting botanicals and other forms of fine art. http://jeannettas-art-gallery.com

Specializing in rare plants, particularly native orchids, in watercolor on vellum, **CAROL WOODIN** has exhibited her art around the world. Her work has been shown most recently at the Museo della Grafica, Pisa, Italy; Santorini Biennale of Arts, Greece; UBS Gallery, New York; and the Shirley Sherwood Gallery, UK. Some collections that include her work are the RBG, Kew; the Smithsonian National Museum of Natural History; the Dr. Shirley Sherwood Collection; and the Alisa and Isaac M. Sutton Collection. Recipient of the 1998 ASBA Diane Bouchier Artist Award and a RHS Gold Medal, she served on the Board of the ASBA, and is now Director of Exhibitions.

After retiring as a professor of art education from Virginia Commonwealth University, **MARY JANE ZANDER** returned to her first love: drawing and painting. Jane believes that botanical art is a great way to satisfy a curious mind. By creating botanical art, the artist also learns about nature and its organization. Like a scientist, the botanical artist observes carefully, and then translates those observations into a visual depiction that captures the "essence" of the plant or object being observed. Jane is President of BASNCR, a member of ASBA, and a teacher at LGBG.

Azure Bluet by Margaret Farr

Index of Flora

Asarum canadense 30
Asclepias incarnata 108
Asimina triloba 80
Baptisia australis 26
Bignonia capreolata 42
Callicarpa americana 14
Cercis canadensis 56
Chionanthus virginicus 126
Clematis ochroleuca 44
Cornus florida 60
Cypripedium acaule 70
Cypripedium kentuckiense 66
Cypripedium reginae 96
Diospyros virginiana 36
Dirca palustris 52
Echinacea purpurea 54
Fothergilla gardenii 50
Galearis spectabilis 98
Goodyera pubescens 48
Hamamelis virginiana 16
Hibiscus moscheutos 40
Houstonia caerulea 18
Hydrangea quercifolia 78
Ilex verticillata 38
Ilex vomitoria & Ilex decidua 130
Jeffersonia diphylla 118
Juglans nigra 22
Kalmia latifolia 72
Kosteletzkya virginica 122
Liatris spicata 46

Lilium superbum 116
Liquidambar styraciflua 110
Liriodendron tulipifera 114
Lobelia cardinalis 32
Magnolia grandiflora 106
Osmunda cinnamomea 34
Osmunda regalis 94
Oxalis montana 74
Polemonium reptans 62
Polygonatum biflorum 102
Pontederia cordata 82
Rhododendron calendulaceum 58
Rhododendron periclymenoides 84
Rhus copallinum 128
Rosa virginiana 120
Rudbeckia hirta 24
Sarracenia purpurea 88
Saururus cernuus 68
Smilax rotundifolia 92
Symplocarpus foetidus 100
Tradescantia virginiana 124
Trillium sessile 112
Typha latifolia 28
Vaccinium corymbosum 64
Viburnum dentatum 104
Viburnum nudum 86
Viola pedata 20
Vitis riparia 90
Vitis rotundifolia 76
Yucca filamentosa 12

Index of Fauna

Abbott's Sphinx moth (*Sphecodina abbottii*) 76
Blue Dasher dragonfly (*Pachydiplax longipennis*) 82, 83
Bordered Patch butterfly (*Chlosyne lacinia*) 25
Bumblebee (*Bombus* spp.) 63
Camouflaged Looper caterpillar (*Synchlora aerata*) 46
Cecropia Silkmoth (*Hyalophora cecropia*) 60
Clouded Sulphur butterfly (*Colias philodice*) 27
Common Buckeye butterfly (*Junonia coenia*) 15
Curve-lined Owlet caterpillar
    (*Phyprosopus callitrichoides*) 92
Curve-lined Owlet moth (*Phyprosopus callitrichoides*) 92
Dufourea novaeangliae bee 83
Eastern Tiger Swallowtail butterfly (*Papilio glaucus*) 55, 115
Goldfinch 46, 54
Gorgone Checkerspot butterfly (*Chlosyne gorgone*) 25
Henry's Elfin butterfly (*Callophrys henrici*) 57, 131
Hickory Horned Devil caterpillar (*Citheronia regalis*) 22
Hummingbird Clearwing moth (*Hemaris thysbe*) 105
Laurel Sphinx moth (*Sphinx kalmiae*) 72
Luna caterpillar (*Actias luna*) 111
Luna moth (*Actias luna*) 22, 37, 111
Monarch butterfly (*Danaus plexippus*) 109
Monarch caterpillar (*Danaus plexippus*) 109
Mourning Cloak butterfly (*Nymphalis antiopa*) 78
Northern Cardinal 92
Northern Bobwhite 15

Painted Lady butterfly (*Vanessa cardui*) 41
Pandorus Sphinx moth (*Eumorpha pandorus*) 91
Pawpaw Sphinx moth (*Dolba hyloeus*) 81, 131
Pipevine Swallowtail butterfly (*Battus philenor*) 58
Queen butterfly (*Danaus gilippus*) 109
Red-banded Hairstreak butterfly (*Calycopis cecrops*) 129
Red-spotted Purple butterfly (*Limenitis arthemis*) 86
Regal Fritillary butterfly (*Speyeria idalia*) 21
Regal Fritillary larva (*Speyeria idalia*) 21
Royal Walnut moth (*Citheronia regalis*) 22
Royal Walnut caterpillar (*Citheronia regalis*) 22
Ruby-throated Hummingbird (*Archilochus colubris*) 33
Rustic Sphinx moth (*Manduca rustica*) 126
Silver-spotted Skipper butterfly (*Epargyreus clarus*) 82, 83
Silvery Checkerspot butterfly (*Chlosyne nycteis*) 25
Small Cabbage White butterfly (*Pieris rapae*) 18, 19
Snowberry Clearwing moth (*Hemaris diffinis*) 109
Spring Azure butterfly (*Celastrina ladon*) 60, 64, 105, 129
Stinging Rose Caterpillar (*Parasa indetermina*) 120
Stinging Rose Moth (*Parasa indetermina*) 120
Tuliptree Silkmoth (*Callosamia angulifera*) 115
Wavy-lined Emerald caterpillar (*Synchlora aerata*) 46
Wavy-lined Emerald moth (*Synchlora aerata*) 46
Yucca Moth (*Tegeticula yuccasella*) 12
Zebra Swallowtail butterfly (*Eurytides marcellus*) 81
Zebra Swallowtail caterpillar (*Eurytides marcellus*) 81

References

Armitage, A. M. 2006. Armitage's Native Plants. Timber Press, Portland, Oregon.

Botany Collections, Smithsonian National Museum of Natural History. http://collections.mnh.si.edu/search/botany/?ti=5 (accessed 2013).

Bracewell, R. N. Trees of Stanford and Environs. Website: Encyclopedia of Trees, Shrubs and Vines. Stanford Historical Society. http://trees.stanford.edu/family.htm (accessed 2013).

Brummit, R. K. 1992. Vascular Plant Families and Genera. Royal Botanic Gardens, Kew. http://data.kew.org/vpfg1992/vascplnt.html (accessed 2013).

Butterflies and Moths of North America (BAMONA). http://www.butterfliesandmoths.org/ (accessed 2013).

Common Names of Insects Database. Entomological Society of America. http://www.entsoc.org/common-names?title=luna+moth&field_sciname_value=&tid=&tid_1=&tid_2=&tid_3=&tid_4= (accessed 2013).

Dirr, M. A. 2009. Manual of Woody Landscape Plants. Stipes Publishing, LLC, Champaign, Illinois.

Eickwort, G. C., P. F. Kukuk, F. R. Wesley. The Nesting Biology of *Dufourea novaeangliae* (Hymenoptera: Halictidae) and the Systematic Position of the Dufoureinae Based on Behavior and Development. Journal of the Kansas Entomological Society 59(1), 1986: 103 -120. http://www.jstor.org/discover/10.2307/25084743?uid=3739256&uid=2129&uid=2&uid=70&uid=4&sid=21102613434693 (accessed 2013).

Gardening Help. Missouri Botanical Garden Plant Information. http://www.missouribotanicalgarden.org/gardens-gardening/your-garden/help-for-the-home-gardener.aspx (accessed 2013).

Gracie, Carol. 2012. Spring Wildflowers of the Northeast: A Natural History. Princeton University Press, Princeton.

Hamel, P. B., and M. U. Chiltoskey. 1975. Cherokee Plants and Their Uses—A 400 Year History. Herald Publishing Co., Sylva, NC.

Herrick, J. W. 1977. Iroquois Medical Botany. State University of New York, Albany, PhD Thesis.

Klein, A. M., B. E. Vaissiere, J. H. Cane, I. Steffan-Dewenter, et al. 2006. Importance of Pollinators in Changing Landscapes for World Crops. Proceedings of the Royal Society: Biological Sciences. U. S. National Library of Medicine, National Institutes of Health. http://www.ncbi.nlm.nih.gov/pmc/articles/PMC1702377/ (accessed 2013).

Kral, R., A. R. Diamond, S. L. Ginzbarg, C. J. Hansen, R. R. Haynes, B. R. Keener, M. G. Lelong, D. D. Spaulding, and M. Woods. 2013. Alabama Plant Atlas. [S.M. Landry and K.N. Campbell (original application development), Florida Center for Community Design and Research. University of South Florida]. University of West Alabama, Livingston, Alabama. http://www.floraofalabama.org/Family.aspx?id+222 (accessed 2013).

Maryland Native Plant Society. http://www.mdflora.org/ (accessed 2013).

McNeill, J., et al. 2012. International Code of Nomenclature for algae, fungi, and plants (Melbourne Code). International Association for Plant Taxonomy. http://www.iapt-taxon.org/nomen/main.php (accessed 2013).

Moerman, D. 1998. Native American Ethnobotany Database. http://herb.umd.umich.edu (accessed 2013).

Native Plant Information Network, NPIN (2013). Lady Bird Johnson Wildflower Center at the University of Texas, Austin, TX. http://www.wildflower.org/plants (accessed 2013).

Ottesen, C. 1995. The Native Plant Primer. Harmony Books, New York.

Perry, M. J. 1975. Food Use of "Wild" Plants by Cherokee Indians. The University of Tennessee, MS Thesis.

Poling, B., and C. Fisk. 2006. Muscadine Grapes in the Home Garden. Department of Horticultural Science, North Carolina State University. http://www.ces.ncsu.edu/hil/hil-8203.html (accessed 2013).

Smith, H. H. 1928. Ethnobotany of the Meskwaki Indians. Bulletin of the Public Museum of the City of Milwaukee 4:175-326.

Speck, F. G. 1941. A List of Plant Curatives Obtained From the Houma Indians of Louisiana. Primitive Man 14:49-75.

Spira, T. P. 2011. Wildflowers & Plant Communities. The University of North Carolina Press, Chapel Hill, North Carolina.

Stevens, P. F. Version 12, July 2012. Angiosperm Phylogeny Website. http://www.mobot.org/MOBOT/research/APweb/ (accessed 2013).

Tantaquidgeon, Gladys. 1972. Folk Medicine of the Delaware and Related Algonkian Indians. Harrisburg, Pennsylvania Historical Commission Anthropological Papers.

Taylor, L. A. 1940. Plants Used As Curatives by Certain Southeastern Tribes. Botanical Museum of Harvard University, Cambridge, MA.

Tropicosorg. Missouri Botanical Garden. http://www.tropicos.org (accessed 2013).

The United States National Arboretum. http://www.usna.usda.gov (accessed 2013).

University of Wisconsin–Madison/ Botany Plant Growth Facilities. University of Wisconsin, Madison. http://www.botany.wisc.edu/plantgrowthfacilities (accessed 2013).

USDA, ARS, National Genetic Resources Program. Germplasm Resources Information Network - (GRIN). National Germplasm Resources Laboratory, Beltsville, Maryland. http://www.ars-grin.gov/cgi-bin/npgs/acc/display.pl?1080421 (accessed September 2013).

USDA, NRCS. 2013. The PLANTS Database. National Plant Data Team, Greensboro, NC 27401-4901 USA. http://plants.usda.gov (accessed 2013).

Virginia Native Plant Society. http://vnps.org/wp/growing-natives (accessed 2013).

Weakley, A. S., J. C. Ludwig, J. F. Townsend, et al. 2012. The Flora of Virginia. Botanical Research Institute of Texas, Fort Worth.

Abbreviations

APG	Angiosperm Phylogeny Group
ASBA	American Society of Botanical Artists
BASNCR	Botanical Art Society of the National Capital Region
BAEE	Botanical Artists for Education & the Environment
CLOS	Central Louisiana Orchid Society
LGBG	Lewis Ginter Botanical Gardens
NESBA	New England Society of Botanical Artists
NRCS	Natural Resources Conservation Service
NYBG	New York Botanical Garden
PSBI	Philadelphia Society of Botanical Illustrators
RBG	Royal Botanic Garden
RHS	Royal Horticultural Society
USBG	United States Botanic Garden
USDA	United States Department of Agriculture

DISCLAIMER: The information contained in this book is for general information and educational purposes only. BAEE makes no claims to the edibility or medicinal use or effect of any plants or flowers, and any information in the book is not a substitute for "professional medical" advice or diagnosis. BAEE does not warrant or assume any legal liability for any information disclosed in the book.

Images in this book originated from a variety of photographic and scanning sources. While we used the best practices and technologies to achieve high-quality, pleasing color reproductions, some colors cannot be exactly reproduced. Neither the publisher, editor, nor authors can be held responsible for differences between the reproductions and the original paintings.